U.S. Military Power and Rapid Deployment Requirements in the 1980s

Westview Replica Editions

The concept of Westview Replica Editions is a response to the continuing crisis in academic and informational publishing. Library budgets for books have been severely curtailed. Ever larger portions of general library budgets are being diverted from the purchase of books and used for data banks, computers, micromedia, and other methods of information retrieval. Interlibrary loan structures further reduce the edition sizes required to satisfy the needs of the scholarly community. Economic pressures on the university presses and the few private scholarly publishing companies have severely limited the capacity of the industry to properly serve the academic and research communities. As a result, many manuscripts dealing with important subjects, often representing the highest level of scholarship, are no longer economically viable publishing projects--or, if accepted for publication, are typically subject to lead times ranging from one to three years.

Westview Replica Editions are our practical solution to the problem. We accept a manuscript in camera-ready form, typed according to our specifications, and move it immediately into the production process. As always, the selection criteria include the importance of the subject, the work's contribution to scholarship, and its insight, originality of thought, and excellence of exposition. The responsibility for editing and proofreading lies with the author or sponsoring institution. We prepare chapter headings and display pages, file for copyright, and obtain Library of Congress Cataloging in Publication Data. A detailed manual contains simple instructions for preparing the final typescript, and our editorial staff is always available to answer questions.

The end result is a book printed on acid-free paper and bound in sturdy library-quality soft covers. We manufacture these books ourselves using equipment that does not require a lengthy make-ready process and that allows us to publish first editions of 300 to 600 copies and to reprint even smaller quantities as needed. Thus, we can produce Replica Editions quickly and can keep even very specialized books in print as long as there is a demand for them.

About the Book and Author

U.S. Military Power and Rapid Deployment Requirements in the 1980s
Sherwood S. Cordier

This book assesses U.S. military needs in the coming decade, focusing on the role of rapid deployment forces in protecting U.S. interests abroad. Dr. Cordier begins by discussing two general developments crucial to future military requirements: first, increasing U.S. dependence on the global sea-lanes as links to key markets; and second, improved Soviet naval, airborne, and sealift capabilities that allow the U.S.S.R. to play an intervention role in the Third World. Given these trends, the most serious U.S. military shortcoming, says Dr. Cordier, is in the area of rapid deployment requirements, particularly lack of sufficient means to transport troops by air and sea to major theaters around the world. Carrier-based airpower and the need for medium-sized aircraft carriers are especially crucial. The book concludes with specific policy recommendations designed to improve U.S. rapid deployment forces.

As an independent observer, Dr. Cordier finds a middle course between the policies of the Reagan administration and those of its opponents in Congress. Currently a professor of history at Western Michigan University, he is the author of *The Air and Sea Lanes of the North Atlantic: Their Security in the 1980s*.

U.S. Military Power and Rapid Deployment Requirements in the 1980s

---

Sherwood S. Cordier

Westview Press / Boulder, Colorado

A Westview Replica Edition

Copyright © 1983 by Westview Press, Inc.

Published in 1983 in the United States of America by
    Westview Press, Inc.
    5500 Central Avenue
    Boulder, Colorado 80301
    Frederick A. Praeger, President and Publisher

Library of Congress Catalog Card Number: 83-50065
ISBN 0-86531-968-5

Printed and bound in the United States of America.

10 9 8 7 6 5 4 3 2 1

Contents

Acknowledgments

A leave of absence, granted by Western Michigan University, helped make this study possible. It is a pleasure to thank the Margaret Burnham Macmillan Fund and the Office of the Dean of the College of Arts and Sciences for partial financial assistance. The valuable services of a research assistant were underwritten by the Graduate College.

Valuable assistance in this study was provided by the Center for Naval Analyses and its Director, Bradford Dismukes. Discussions with Herschel Kanter, Colonel John R. Landry (USA), Michael MccGwire, Michael Moodie, Stephen E. Ockenden and Commander Bruce W. Watson (USN) proved stimulating and enlightening. Only the author, of course, is responsible for the data and views to be found in this volume.

The professional skills of Mrs. Judith Massie, who typed the manuscript, and Michael and Kimberly Winblad, who set the final copy by word processor, are warmly appreciated. I am grateful to my wife, Mary, whose encouragement and support during the throes of authorship have meant so much.

Sherwood S. Cordier
March 1983

I

Introduction

The naval forces of the United States are now at a crucial juncture in their historical development. A host of problems have sapped the strength of the fleet that ruled supreme over the oceans of the world in the era following the Second World War. Many ships of World War II vintage have been retired. Other warships, brought into service in the 1950s, will soon reach the end of their useful life. The lean budget years of the 1970s have failed to replace the numbers of ships and aircraft lost to the Navy. Naval operations are hamstrung by a dire shortage of highly skilled technicians and experienced non-commissioned officers.

However, while U.S. naval capabilities have considerably eroded, the responsibilities confronting the United States Navy have substantially increased. Seaborne trade, upon which the economy of the United States depends, has burgeoned. Dependence upon overseas sources of indispensable minerals has grown by a quantum degree. In the 1950s Russia possessed little more than a coastal defense fleet. Today the Soviet Union can boast a true high seas navy, capable of operating in any far flung corner of the world. However, as the Iranian Crisis and the Falkland Islands War clearly demonstrate, challenges other than Soviet abound in the world. The spread of massive quantities of sophisticated weaponry ensures that virtually all nations now enjoy substantial lethal arsenals. The predicament of the U.S. Navy is aptly summarized as a one and a half ocean fleet overstretched to cope with responsibilities in three oceans.[1] However, American and western interests in such vital areas as Africa and the Middle East involve all of the armed forces of the United States and a wide range of military capabilities.

The Soviet Union has developed the doctrine, strategy, and forces appropriate to intervention in continents far from the Russian homeland. Key Soviet

1

partners, notably Cuba and East Germany, furnish substantial contingents of troops and military specialists. In the course of the 1970s the Soviets have undertaken successful ventures in Africa and along the Indian Ocean. Again, however, Soviet and Cuban empire building are far from being the only threat to western interests. Internecine conflict among Third World nations and the internal fragility of vital oil and mineral producing regimes pose even graver problems for the United States and its allies. Such problems arise frequently, admit no simple solutions, and can be dauntingly intractable.

Development of U.S. strategies and forces for effective operations in such areas as Africa and the Persian Gulf have been crippled by revulsion against the commitment of the United States in the protracted and costly war in Southeast Asia. In the wake of the Vietnam conflict U.S. military budgets were sharply reduced. During the 1970s the massive expansion and re-equipment of all Soviet armed forces compelled the United States to concentrate its limited funds, resources, and forces in defense of the critical areas of Western Europe and Korea. Other vital areas of the world and the branches of the armed forces relevant to their defense were woefully neglected. Heavy reliance was placed upon such regimes as the former Shah of Iran. A succession of events, culminating in the overthrow of the Shah, the seizure of the American Embassy in Iran, and the Soviet occupation of Afghanistan, shattered this strategic edifice.

It is under these circumstances that the Reagan Administration has embarked upon a 1.6 trillion dollar program designed to remedy glaring armed forces deficiencies and recapture the pinnacle of military superiority once enjoyed by the United States. Appropriately, modernization and expansion of the U.S. Navy takes pride of place in the planned renovation of United States forces. Such an enterprise will exact a high price. To accomplish the goals set forth by naval leadership will entail ship construction costs estimated as high as 183.6 billion dollars over a ten year period.[2] This does not take into account the cost of fuel, ammunition, maintenance, and crew to operate the fleet. To sustain a 600 ship Navy, Michael MccGwire estimates future naval appropriations must run 14.4 billion dollars annually, a figure double that of the past fifteen years.[3]

Attention now also focuses upon those forces which can be brought into action overseas and swiftly. To coordinate the operations of such units a Rapid Deployment Joint Task Force Headquarters was established in 1980. The capabilities of the Marine Corps assume a renewed relevance. The U.S. Army underlines the utility of its airborne and air assault formations. A new light high technology division is in the process of development. The value of forces that can be speedily deployed to far corners of the globe and fight effectively is now highlighted.

Many fundamental questions arise, however, about the direction, scope, and form of the current U.S. military effort. Such concerns are heightened by the present economic depression and the massive federal budget deficits looming on the horizon.

What kind of Navy can best serve U.S. strategic interests? Should the nuclear fueled super aircraft carrier continue to be the capital ship of the fleet? A carrier battle group, comprising the super carrier and six large, heavily armed escorts, costs 17 billion dollars. Indeed, for every dollar spent on a super carrier an additional $7.10 must be expended on escort ships and their sophisticated electronics and weaponry.[4] A vigorous controversy has erupted over the future role of surface fleets.[5] Are major warships too vulnerable to sophisticated missiles and torpedoes?

How can the merchant shipping so vital to western economies be most effectively protected against the depredations of hostile submarines and fast missile boats? How can the new amphibious warfare ships and hovercraft needed to keep the Marines a viable force be secured in the numbers needed? These concerns tend to be overshadowed by the carrier controversy but are no less vital than the capital ship.

Can vertical and short take off and landing warplanes play an increased role in airpower at sea? In the Falkland Islands War British Sea Harrier fighters shot down at least 32 Argentine aircraft with no loss of Harriers in air to air encounters.[6] The British V/STOL machines featured a high 80 percent availability rate and flew some six sorties each day of the conflict.[7] The U.S. Navy is interested in tilt engine patrol aircraft and suitable ships for their deployment.[8]

The commitment of U.S. forces to theatres distant from the homeland is severely constrained by a shortage of transport aircraft and modern sea going freighters. Unhappily, the airlift question was embroiled in a bitter and unedifying congressional duel between Boeing of Washington state and Lockheed of Georgia. Overlooked in the air transport brawl is the even more significant matter of sealift. Since 90 percent of needed war cargo will go by ship it is deplorable indeed to find only 28 U.S. merchant ships in the U.S. Ready Reserve and a total of but 575 freighters and tankers in the U.S. merchant marine.[9] The condition of U.S. sealift may well be the Achilles heel of our conventional capabilities. The British found it necessary to mobilize 54 merchant ships to support their expedition to recapture the Falkland Islands.

What U.S. ground forces are best suited to the rapid deployment role? Should this vital role be exclusively entrusted to the Marine Corps, as Jeffrey Record and others have urged?[10] What part can airborne forces realistically play? How can light forces be effectively armed against enemy tanks and other armor? What light armored vehicles, readily carried by air, can be secured for U.S. units? Helicopters are quite effective in both the transport and "gunship" roles. Can great numbers of helicopters, however, be adequately supplied and maintained in a situation of intense and sustained combat in desert or high plateau?

How can U.S. tactical air strength be brought to bear in remote theatres of the world? Control of the air is the key to successful ground operations in desert or other open terrain. The United States Air Force Tactical Air Command is well equipped with F-15 and F-16 air superiority fighters and A-10 "tank-buster" attack planes. The U.S. Air Force has developed a system of airborne radar tracking of hostile warplanes and direction of friendly fighters to shoot down their foes.

But deploying U.S. airpower to distant arenas is an enormously complicated and costly task. Frequent refuelings in air demand the support of many tanker aircraft. Bases must be established and secured. Even so, tactical airpower is clearly one of the strongest cards the United States can play. As Thomas Etzold emphasizes:

> Since World War II, tactical aviation has provided an answer to one of the most classic puzzles in the history of warfare: how to engage decisively when a great land power and a great sea power meet. Around the periphery of Eurasia, and wherever else this classic collision occurs, tactical aviation has assumed a new and still increasing significance.[11]

In the course of the 1970s the Soviet Union has brought to fruition the doctrine for a strategy of intervention in far reaches of the world and a variety of projection strategies and forces to implement such operations. Carl G. Jacobsen notes:

> The early and mid-1970's saw the publication of a number of Soviet statements evincing new-found appreciation of interventionary prospects in distant areas. The point of departure may have been provided by the 1971 Party Congress and by the emphasis with which General Secretary Brezhnev then reaffirmed Moscow's "duty" to oppose imperialist

aggression and support wars of national liberation.[12]

Soviet tactical aviation has undergone a revolutionary transformation. It is now capable of a wide range of offensive operations. The tactical branch of the Soviet Air Force has been completely equipped with new and advanced warplanes. It will be furnished with an array of even more sophisticated and effective machines in the mid and late 1980s. The expansion of Soviet air transport proceeds apace. Russian Military Transport Aviation has been employed quite successfully in a series of massive airlift operations in Africa and the Middle East. Combat helicopter development has been strongly emphasized. As a result Russia now can boast of more combat helicopters in service than the United States.[13]

Soviet ambitions, however, remain constrained by a very small force of Naval Infantry and a paucity of amphibious assault ships. To surmount this handicap the Soviet Union has developed a strategy of basing ground and air forces, along with immense stockpiles of weapons and equipment, in key African and Middle Eastern countries. An essential ingredient in this strategy is the employment of substantial numbers of Cuban and East German troops. In Angola alone, for example, 18,000 Cuban and 450 East German soldiers and airmen were to be found in July 1982.[14]

Reflecting decisions taken and doctrine developed in the 1960s, the Soviet Navy has developed in the 1970s into a formidable instrument of diplomatic pressure and political influence, particularly in the Third World arena. Peacetime naval diplomacy in support of "the State interests of the USSR in the seas and oceans," as the Russians term it, now ranks among the tasks of the fleet second only to the protection of the strategic missile submarine force in time of war.[15] The Russian fleet, John M. Collins notes, ". . . is routinely used to reap or retain an international reservoir of good will, which Soviet leaders (despite setbacks) try to translate into political persuasion, basing privileges, and other practical products that can have a significant bearing on the US/Soviet balance."[16] In a thorough and very detailed study of Soviet naval operations, Bruce W. Watson concludes:

> Apparently the Soviets believe that naval response to a crisis is an important foreign policy option, and they intend to use such responses to justify bolstering a naval force already stationed in an area, or stationing a force in areas where Soviet naval power has not previously existed.[17]

In the mid-1970s and early 1980s a stream of large
and powerful warships have entered service with the
Soviet fleet. Such ships feature long operating range
and ample stocks of ammunition and other stores. The
array of new Soviet warships includes 44,000 ton VTOL
aircraft carriers, 23,000 ton missile armed battle
cruisers, and 7,800 ton anti-submarine and 8,200 ton
general purpose heavy destroyers.[18] As Michael
MccGwire stresses:

> And naval design criteria have shifted from
> short-term survivability to sustaining combat
> operations for the duration of a war. This
> means that, for the first time, wartime
> requirements will generate a general purpose
> Navy with a true world-wide capability,
> suitable for use as an instrument of state
> policy in peacetime.[19]

A measured view must be taken, however of the
Kremlin's ability to project Soviet power and influence
into distant arenas effectively. The Soviet Union
lacks a number of key tools of long range force
projection, among them carrier based conventional
airpower and respectable amphibious forces and
capabilities. Caution has been the hallmark of Soviet
commitments; the Russians have undertaken operations
only when prospects of success appeared to be high and,
most often, when no American opposition would be
encountered. Even under these circumstances Moscow has
not etched an unblemished record; the Russians have
suffered some singular reverses. The Soviets were
virtually evicted from Egypt. Ensnared in regional
internecine rivalries, the Russians were compelled to
disavow their Somalian client and abruptly switch to
the defense of Ethiopia, losing one of the finest
natural harbors of the Indian Ocean, Berbera, in the
process.
      Yet the Soviet Union is no longer solely a
continental power confined to the steppes of Eurasia.
Now the Soviet Union has emerged upon the world stage
as a truly global power.
      Moreover the growing Soviet role in world affairs
goes hand in glove with the rapidly expanding
integration of the USSR into the world economy. Soviet
dependence upon other countries for essential supplies
of grain and animal feed is well known. Sugar, fruit,
coffee, tea, and cocoa must also be secured from
foreign sources. Although the Soviet Union is
immensely rich in a wide array of vital minerals, the
Russians have become increasingly dependent upon
foreign suppliers for critical raw materials. As Keith
A. Dunn points out:

. . . it imports all its sheet mica needed to
make critical electronic appliances. . . .
Moscow has imported larger quantities of
beryllium for toughening metal, tantalum for
use in electronic components, and lithium
needed in aluminum production.[20]

It is true that the Soviet Union is the largest oil
producer in the world and that immense oil riches are
to be found in the Arctic reaches of that vast land.
But it is very difficult and costly to tap the oil in
these inhospitable areas far removed from the
industrial centers where it can be refined and
consumed. To be sure, the Kremlin will take every
measure to assure continued Soviet self-sufficiency in
such a crucial component of military strength. But it
may well prove difficult for the Russians to maintain
exports of oil, the main earner of indispensable
foreign hard currency. Moscow needs such hard currency
to pay the interest on the enormous debts the eastern
bloc has accrued to western banks and governments, as
well as to purchase advanced technology from western
firms. It may indeed be impossible for the Soviet
Union to supply the oil needs of its Eastern European
satellite nations. Already Soviet tankers bring oil
from Iraq to Eastern European refineries.
In the light of these considerations it is
imperative that a fundamental transformation be wrought
in U.S. strategy. To be sure the United States must
cope with the Soviet challenge. But U.S. strategy may
well be fixed upon the contingency of nuclear conflict
while the very basis of our economy is being eroded day
by day. We stand in danger of investing heavily in
forces and weapons that may prove to be costly,
vulnerable, and from a strategic standpoint, profoundly
irrelevant. A case in point is a U.S. surface Navy
whose centerpiece, to the exclusion of much else, is
the super carrier.
While U.S. attention is mesmerized by the specter
of global and nuclear confrontation, the Soviet Union
gains greater ability to threaten the sealanes upon
which the western economies depend and undermines the
western position in the mineral-rich areas of Africa
and the Middle East. Whether such a strategy is the
result of brilliant Soviet malice aforethought is a
matter of controversy. It may be that the Kremlin,
exploiting opportune circumstances, fell into an
operational mode offering such remarkable potential.
Whatever the case may be, the long range impact upon
the United States and its western and east Asian allies
could be disastrous.
U.S. strategy has far too long been hypnotized by
the Soviet threat and by the yardstick of cost
effectiveness, the management model so dominant in U.S.

society. Such approaches are valuable for assessing
the capabilities of rivals in the world and for
implementing strategy, but they cannot be a substitute
for strategic analysis. Spending vast sums for "more
of the same" kinds of forces and weapons may wreak
great harm upon U.S. military capabilities.

The U.S. Navy must meet the day to day continuous
demands of commerce upon the high seas. The United
States is tightly interwoven in a mutually
interdependent world economy. U.S. dependence on
imported oil is well known. The Congressional Budget
Office has estimated that a cut off of oil from Saudi
Arabia for one year would boost an already high U.S.
unemployment rate by two percent and send inflation
soaring by 20 percent.[21] On the other side of the coin,
exports from the United States in 1979 accounted for 70
percent of the world market in corn, 45 percent in
wheat, 40 percent in steel scrap, and 34 percent in
coal.[22]

Navies should also help assure an uninterrupted
flow of critically needed raw materials. The United
States must now import in excess of 50 percent of 23 of
40 crucial minerals. The U.S. Defense Science Board
states that U.S. dependence upon imports is 100 percent
for columbian, mica, and titanium, 93 percent for
bauxite, and 90 percent for chromium and cobalt.[23]
These vital elements come from every corner of the
globe: Brazil, India, Australia, Thailand, South
Africa, Zimbabwe, Zambia, and Zaire.

Navies and amphibious forces are indispensable
means to exert influence where vital interests are at
stake. Most ground forces depend upon the fleet for
overseas deployment. Troops and tactical air must rely
upon the Navy to protect long supply lines and
guarantee the continued flow of ammunition, fuel,
equipment, food, and water.

Powers of the second and third rank have now built
up formidable armories of sophisticated weapons and
substantial armed forces. Bitter rivalries abound in
critical areas of the world. Quite a number of such
regimes are internally vulnerable and violently
unstable.

Navies are particularly well suited to bring to
bear a flexible and subtle influence on behalf of
stability and gradual change. The peaceful uses of
naval power should be emphasized -- peacekeeping
deterrence. Violence must be kept at the lowest level
of the spectrum of conflict. Stress should be upon the
minimal use of force and the maximum employment of
diplomacy -- and navies can be an excellent tool of
diplomacy.

An analysis of naval strategy must take into
account the profound impact of the balance of power on
land upon the maritime balance at sea. Even Great

. Britain, a classic maritime power, intervened frequently over three centuries in European affairs to secure a continental balance of power favorable to her interests. If, for instance, Iran should fall into the Soviet camp and make air bases available to Russian forces U.S. naval units in the Indian Ocean would be hard pressed indeed. Loss of key U.S. air and naval bases in the Philippines would severely handicap U.S. seapower in southeast Asia and the Indian Ocean.

Under these circumstances it is essential to emphasize the necessary and complementary cooperation of sea, land, and tactical air forces. No service can operate solo. Moreover, the impact of modern technology is outlined by Michael Moodie:

> As technological developments expand the range of action of new weapons systems, forces on land can exert a control of the sea undreamed of in Admiral Nelson's or even Admiral Mahan's day. Conversely, naval forces can strike more deeply against land targets and bring more power to bear in a crisis on the shore than those two naval strategists could have ever imagined. There is no longer a choice between land power and seapower; the two are closely related.[24]

Although clearly necessary, cooperation among the armed forces is difficult to implement in practice. Interservice rivalry is a well known factor. Such rivalry is honed to a sharp edge by stiff competition for scarce military budget funds. Thus fundamental strategic decisions cannot be wholly entrusted to the military services.

It should be clear that the United States cannot "go it alone" in the world. Rich as the United States is, it possesses neither the resources nor the wealth to pursue a strategy of unilateral action and isolation. At the pinnacle of their imperial career, even the British found a policy of "splendid isolation" to be bankrupt, and were compelled to seek allies in the early years of this century. The U.S. economy is completely enmeshed in the wider context of a world economic order. The economy of the United States depends upon a stream of imported raw materials and the outward flow of exports to foreign markets.

Necessarily, a fundamental feature of U.S. policy must be a coalition strategy. Only a combination of powers sharing similar values can hope to cope with a disorderly and eruptive world. However much the U.S. may quarrel with its Western European and Far Eastern allies it must be recognized that such frictions are family arguments. Our key partners do make considerable contributions in key corners of the world.

France maintains substantial ground forces designed for rapid deployment and French troops are committed to a number of African countries. Great Britain has demonstrated the ability to mount a successful major military operation 8,000 miles from home waters. In Southeast Asia Australian and New Zealand forces play a significant role. Even Japan is beginning to take up a larger share in military responsibility in the Far East, with the approval of a 65.6 billion dollar five year program of defense expenditures.[25] Japan will possess a large force of anti-submarine patrol aircraft and a fighter arm equipped with F-15s.

A coalition strategy is the logical strategic corollary to the world economy in which the United States is interwoven. It would also reflect the wide range of political values and human concerns that knit the United States and its allies together. A flexible, versatile, and multi-purpose U.S. Navy can be the backbone of such an effective coalition strategy.

1. Thomas B. Hayward (Admiral, USN, Chief of Naval Operations), Hearings before the U.S. Senate Committee on Armed Services on the Department of Defense Authorization for Appropriations for Fiscal year 1981, 96th Congress, 2d session, part 2 (Washington, D.C.: U.S. Government Printing Office, 1980), p. 785.

2. Douglas D. Mitchell, Shipbuilding Costs For General Purpose Forces In a 600-Ship Navy (Washington, D.C.: Congressional Research Service, Library of Congress, February 16, 1982), p. 9.

3. Michael MccGwire, Six Hundred Ships: The Navy and National Security, part II: The Cost (Unpublished Draft, April 1982), p. 14.

4. Mitchell, p. 11.

5. Richard Halloran (New York Times), "Warships' future uncertain," Seattle Post-Intelligencer, 12 July 1982, p. A9.

6. "British Harriers Average Six Sorties Per Day," Aviation Week & Space Technology, 19 July 1982, pp. 20-21.

7. Ibid.

8. "Service Revives Interest in V/STOL," Aviation Week & Space Technology, 21 September 1981, pp. 70-74.

9. Deborah M. Kyle, "Sealift," Armed Forces Journal International, July 1982, p. 57.

10. Jeffrey Record, The Rapid Deployment Force and U.S. Military Intervention in the Persian Gulf, (Cambridge, Massachusetts: Institute For Foreign Policy Analysis, Inc., February 1982), p. 69.

11. Thomas H. Etzold, "Responding to Soviet Intervention in the Third World," Naval War College Review, volume 35, May-June 1982, p. 32.

12. Carl G. Jacobsen, Soviet Strategic Initiatives: Challenge and Response (New York, New York: Praeger Publishers, 1979), p. 14.

13 Deborah G. Meyer, "What's in the Soviet Helicopter Arsenal?" Armed Forces Journal International, May 1982, p. 42.

14. The International Institute for Strategic Studies, The Military Balance: 1982-1983 (London, Great Britain: The International Institute for

Strategic Studies, 1982), p. 66.

15. Jacobsen, p. 16.

16. John M. Collins, U.S.-Soviet Military Balance: Concepts and Capabilities, 1960-1980 (New York, New York: McGraw-Hill Publications Co., 1980), p. 245.

17. Bruce W. Watson, Red Navy at Sea: Soviet Naval Operations on the High Seas, 1956-1980, (Boulder, Colorado: Westview Press, 1982), p. 171.

18. Jean Labayle Couhat, ed., Combat Fleets Of The World 1982/83: Their Ships, Aircraft, and Armament (Annapolis, Maryland: The United States Naval Institute, 1982). pp. 593-596, 616-619, and 628-631.

19. Michael MccGwire, "A New Trend in Soviet Naval Developments," International Defense Review, Number 5, 1980, p. 677.

20. Keith A. Dunn, "Strategy, The Soviet Union And The 1980's," Naval War College Review, volume 34, September-October 1981, p. 21.

21. David A. Deese and Joseph S. Nye, editors, Energy And Security (Cambridge, Massachusetts: Ballinger Publishing Company, 1981), p. 3.

22. The United Nations, Yearbook of International Trade Statistics, volume II (New York, New York: The United Nations, 1981), pp. passim.

23. The International Institute for Strategic Studies, Strategic Survey 1981-1982 (London, Great Britain: The International Institute for Strategic Studies, 1982), p. 44.

24. Michael Moodie and Alvin J. Cottrell, Geopolitics and Maritime Power (Beverly Hills, California: Sage Publications, 1981), p. 17.

25. "Japanese Defense Council Approves Five-Year Plan," Aviation Week & Space Technology, 9 August 1982, p. 96.

II
The Web of Interdependence: The United States in a World Economy

Never before in history have so much of the world's goods moved across the high seas. Seaborne trade has been vastly magnified by modern technology. Present day freighters dwarf their predecessors. Oil tankers in particular are truly gigantic. Modern ships are swift, moving two or three times the speed of ships of earlier vintage. New merchantmen are highly automated, requiring crews quite skilled but minimum in number. They are outfitted with equipment for convenient loading of cargo in large containers and can disgorge their goods rapidly at dockside.

Little wonder that at least two-thirds of total world trade by value is shipborne.[1] Nor should it be surprising that ship transits of general cargo and petroleum are expected to virtually double from 1974 to 1985.[2] Under these circumstances leading sealanes are crowded with traffic. An unbroken stream of ships passes through the English Channel every day. A steady procession of oil tankers sail around the Cape of Good Hope into the South Atlantic en route to refineries in Western Europe and North America. Some 26,000 merchant ships sail around the South African Cape every year.[3]

The salient role of the United States in the world economy is clearly illustrated by the immense array of commodities exported and imported by this country. In 1979, 70 percent of total world exports in corn came from the United States, 45 percent of the wheat, 33 percent of the rice, and 26 percent of the animal feed.[4] Flowing from the United States were: 40 percent of total world exports in steel scrap, 34 percent of coal, 27 percent of timber, and 22 percent of fertilizers.[5] It is an impressive sight to view hundreds of freighters stretching to the far horizon at Hampton Roads, Virginia, waiting to carry U.S. coal to distant markets.

The import side of the trade ledger in 1979 showed the United States leading the world in the purchase of bauxite, tungsten, zinc, and tin.[6] Imports of iron ore

and chromium placed the United States second only to
Japan. The United States was on the heels of West
Germany in consumption of foreign aluminum, copper,
silver, and platinum.[7]

Not all of these goods come and go overseas. Much
trade passes across the borders of Canada and Mexico.
But the major markets for key U.S. exports are to be
found overseas. Moreover, a wide range of critical
minerals must come by water from South America, Africa,
and Southeast Asia.

Oil -- the lifeblood of western and Japanese
economies -- is the most striking example of a largely
seaborne crucial natural resource. In 1978, according
to Charles Perry, petroleum accounted for 47 percent of
the total energy supply in the United States, 58
percent in Western Europe, and 72 percent in Japan.[8]
Western Europe in 1978 imported 87 percent of its oil
requirements and Japan 99.8 percent of its petroleum
needs.[9]

The United States has reduced its dependence on
imported oil from 46 percent in 1977 to 32 percent in
1981.[10] But the decline in U.S. imports resulted from
conservation and the impact of the recession. Charles
J. DiBona asserts that:

> None of the independent estimates suggest that
> we are going to see a significant increase in
> the amount of oil and gas found in the United
> States. We will be doing quite well to
> essentially hold at today's level of
> production.[11]

Even though more oil wells were drilled in the United
States in 1981 than in any previous year, petroleum
production failed to register any significant gain.[12]

Certain areas of the world play singularly
prominent roles in the supply of petroleum. The oil
producing nations of the Persian Gulf are a case in
point. In 1980 the United States secured 28.8 percent
of its imported oil from Persian Gulf countries,
Western Europe 58.9 percent, and Japan 72.9 percent.[13]
The states of West Africa have recently emerged as
increasingly important oil suppliers. Great Britain,
Norway, Denmark, and West Germany have drawn heavily
upon the oil fields of the North Sea. The United
States now imports more oil from Latin America than
heretofore. Yet, as Charles Perry emphasizes:

> Without secure access to the petroleum
> supplies of the Persian Gulf and West Africa,
> and to the logistical facilities and regional
> sea lanes necessary for their transportation,
> the United States and its industrial allies
> would face the prospect of crippling energy

shortages. Judging from current and projected
trends in oil demand and supply, together with
the slow development of alternative energy
sources, this is likely to remain the case for
at least the next decade.[14]

Dependence by the United States, Western Europe, and
Japan upon imported minerals and metals is even more
critical than their reliance upon petroleum. Western
European countries are overwhelmingly dependent upon
African sources for a wide array of raw materials.[15]
Japan secures quantities of resources from East Asia,
particularly Australia. Canada and Latin America help
meet the mineral needs of the United States. Even so
the United States is heavily dependent upon Central and
Southern African states for the supply of very critical
minerals.
     Moreover, domestic sources for minerals and metals
from overseas are by no means readily available. The
difficulties are succinctly outlined by Charles Perry:

     . . . the processing technology of industrial
     users may be primed to accept only certain
     grades or forms of feedstock minerals and a
     switch to supplies from another country may
     require expensive and time-consuming retooling
     and adaptation. . . . domestic substitution
     among mineral consumers in the industrial
     world requres . . . large capital costs and
     significant lead times. . . . substitution
     efforts require near monumental programs of
     national economic mobilization that very few
     countries are willing to bear, except in
     wartime conditions.[16]

Compounding the problem is the fact that highly
sophisticated technologies, particularly in electronics
and metal alloys, demand a quantum increase in certain
key minerals and rare earths. In order to conserve
energy, new high strength and light weight metal alloys
have been developed -- but these also are made from
certain metal ores.
     To be sure, the United States maintains stockpiles
of strategic raw materials. However such stockpiles
are incomplete and inadequate. Holdings are but half
the required amount in 23 of the 61 groups of
materials.[17] Only 48 percent of the needed cobalt
inventory exists and but 33 percent of the minimum
needed tantalum is stockpiled.[18] Many would require
extensive processing to be industrially usable. Worst
of all, stockpile requirements were drawn up years ago
and fall far short of meeting the demands of current
and future technology. Some of the newest vital
elements, especially in electronics, are not even

listed for stockpiling.

Over the period 1975-1981 the United States Defense
Science Board has charted U.S. dependence upon
critical minerals. In materials vital to electronics,
the United States is 100 percent dependent on imports
of sheet mica and 96 percent dependent on tantalum
imports.[19] The percentages of U.S. imports of metal
ores are: titanium, 100 percent; manganese, 98
percent; chromium, 90 percent; and cobalt, 90
percent.[20]

Fortunately, most of the titanium is secured from
Australia. Sheet mica and tantalum are primarily
purchased from India, Thailand, and Malaysia. But the
main sources of chromium, cobalt, and manganese are the
unstable and sensitive areas of Central and Southern
Africa, notably Gabon, South Africa, Zaire, Zimbabwe,
and Zambia.

Why are these minerals so critically important?
Cobalt and columbium are absolutely necessary in the
fabrication of key elements of computers and of
military electronics, particularly avionic systems,
electronic countermeasures equipment, and the new
generation of superconductors. To belabor the obvious,
electronic systems and computers are assuming an
increasingly dominant role in the way of life,
economies, and military systems of countries everywhere
in the world.

Cobalt is also indispensable in the heat resistant
superalloys employed in the high performance jet
engines that power civil airliners and warplanes.
Titanium is a vital component of the ultra high
strength and lightweight alloy used in the structure of
high performance warplanes and submarines. Much more
widespread is the utilization of chrome in stainless
steel and a variety of nonferrous steel alloys. So
important is chrome that, according to the Foreign
Ministry of West Germany, a 30 percent slash in chrome
imports for a year would entail the loss of seven
million jobs and reduce industrial production in West
Germany by one-quarter.[21] Manganese is an element in
almost all steels. It is also essential in dry cell
batteries. There are no substitutes for manganese. As
the American Geological Institute incisively sums up:

> Without manganese, chromium, platinum, and
> cobalt, there can be no automobiles, no
> airplanes, no jet engines, no satellites, and
> no sophisticated weapons -- not even home
> appliances.[22]

The United States is thus a maritime nation, a
giant island, whose links with key markets and mineral
sources are oceanborne. The first purposes of a U.S.
Navy are thus dictated by maritime needs. A

flourishing U.S. economy and viable polity are based on an unhampered use of the global sealanes. An uninterrupted flow of needed oil and other minerals can only be assured by the development, and deployment into action if need be, of suitable air and ground units drawn from all the armed forces.

18

1. Paul H Nitze, Leonard Sullivan, Jr., and the Atlantic Council Working Group on Securing the Seas, Securing the Seas: The Soviet Naval Challenge and Western Alliance Options (Boulder, Colorado: Westview Press, 1979), p. 132.

2. Ibid., pp. 132, 136.

3. Moodie and Cottrell, p. 37.

4 The United Nations, Yearbook of International Trade Statistics.

5. Ibid.

6. Ibid.

7. Ibid.

8. Charles Perry, The West, Japan and Cape Route Imports: The Oil And Non-Fuel Mineral Trades (Cambridge, Massachusetts: Institute For Foreign Policy Analysis, Inc., 1982), p. 4.

9. Ibid.

10. Stan Benjamin, Newhouse News Service, "Energy crisis lurks behind the scenes," Kalamazoo Gazette, 27 December 1981, p. G-3.

11. Ibid.

12. Robert Burns, The Associated Press, "America's not out of the oil-crises woods yet," The Ledger (Lakeland, Florida), 26 February 1982, p. 1.

13. Perry, p. 8.

14. Ibid., p. 45.

15. Ibid., p. 61.

16. Ibid., p. 48.

17. The International Institute for Strategic Studies, Strategic Survey 1981-1982, p. 43.

18. Ibid.

19. Ibid., p. 44.

20. Ibid.

19

21.   Perry, p. 65.

22.   Council on Economics and National Security, <u>Strategic Minerals: A Resource Crisis</u> (New York, New York: National Strategy Information Center, 1981), p. 8.

III
Intervention in the Third World: Soviet Doctrine and Operations

Soviet ambitions to play a role on the global stage are not new found. Indeed such aspirations are rooted deep in Soviet history. But the USSR was preoccupied with internal industrial development in the late 1920s and through the 1930s. Then the Soviet Union fought for its very existence in the Second World War. Not until the devastation wrought by the war was repaired could the Russians take up the quest for a world role. The path to such a position has been long, beset by difficulties, and marked by daunting setbacks.

As is usually the case with Soviet policy, a concept by Lenin provides a key to understanding the fundamental Russian approach in foreign affairs. In a lecture on December 6, 1920 Lenin, as Bruce Watson points out:

> . . . noted five antagonisms that would endure for decades. The first three -- the United States vs. Japan, the United States vs. Europe, and Europe vs. Germany -- were resolved, at least temporarily, by World War II. The fourth was between the colonial powers and their colonies. . . . he implied that conflicts would occur in the colonial empires and that the Soviet Union should stand as defender of the world's oppressed peoples. Dissolution of the colonial empires also would weaken the "imperialist powers" and hasten the socialist revolution.[1]

Lenin advised that the fifth conflict, between the capitalist world and the new Russian regime, be soft pedalled, the better to exploit the other rivalries for Soviet purposes. Lenin's view casts a long and illuminating shaft of light upon the context of Soviet purpose and policy.

In a detailed analysis of the evolution of Soviet doctrine, James M. McConnell demonstrates that: "Most

21

of the key decisions involved in the new approach to the Third World were made in the half decade at the turn of the Stalinist and post-Stalinist eras."[2] Such decisions include the opening of trade with the non-Communist world in 1951. Soviet economic aid to selected institutions and countries soon followed in 1953. 1955 saw the conclusion of an arms agreement with Egypt. In 1956, as Bruce Watson emphasizes, the Twentieth Party Congress set aside special funds for the construction of a high seas fleet, to be under the leadership of the very able Admiral Sergei G. Gorshkov.[3] Simultaneously, a tremendous expansion of the fishing and merchant fleets was set in motion.

By the 1960s the Kremlin could take a most fundamental step in the formulation of a doctrine of intervention in the Third World, the definition of local war and a willingness to take up arms in such limited conflicts under certain conditions. An array of articles and statements, particularly in 1965-1966, elaborate the local war concept.[4] The Soviet commitment to such struggles, in appropriate circumstances, was voiced by Colonel N. Zagorodnikov:

> The armed forces of the socialist commonwealth assist in a resolute manner the independent development of peoples who have liberated themselves from the colonial yoke, and they prevent the export of counter-revolution into countries that are carrying out an independent and peaceloving policy.[5]

Linked with the willingness of Moscow to intervene actively in Third World affairs was a new found appreciation of African and Asian military regimes. The toppling of the "progressive" Nkrumah government of Ghana in 1966 wrought a sharp change in Soviet policy toward military dictatorships. As Charles C. Petersen notes:

> . . . as radical officers seized power in a number of countries, Soviet hopes came to rest on left-wing military rule not only for the political stability it seemed to guarantee, but also for the momentum it seemed to impart to the revolutionary process. Military stewardship came to be viewed as an often inevitable stage along the path to a socialist order.[6]

It is during the 1960s, moreover, that Cuba, the nation which was to become the Kremlin's major partner in Third World ventures, emerged upon the African stage. As William J. Durch stresses:

Havana has aided "progressive" regimes and revolutionary movements in Africa at least since 1961. Cuban military advisers fought with guerrilla groups in Zaire and Portuguese Guinea in the 1960's, and trained the "peoples militias" of a number of countries between 1965 and 1977.[7]

Thus did the so-called "surrogate" or "proxy" strategy emerge in the course of the 1960s.

In the 1970s Soviet interventionary doctrine came to full maturity. In 1972, an especially incisive statement emanated from a leading theorist, V.M. Kulish:

> Military support must be furnished to those nations fighting for their freedom. . . . The Soviet Union may require mobile and well trained and well equipped armed forces. . . . The actual situation may require the Soviet Union to carry out measures aimed at restraining the aggressive acts of imperialism . . . expanding the scale of Soviet military presence and military assistance furnished by other socialist states are being viewed today as a very important factor in international relations.[8]

In 1974 General Andrei A. Grechko, then Minister of Defense, expressed the Soviet view with utter clarity:

> At the present stage the historic function of the Armed Forces is not restricted merely to their function in defending our Motherland and the other socialist countries. In its foreign policy activity the Soviet state actively purposefully opposes the export of counter-revolution and the policy of oppression, supports the national liberation struggle, and resolutely resists imperialistic aggression in whatever distant region of our planet it may appear.[9]

The imprimatur of Communist Party approval appeared in a series of statements by Leonid Brezhnev culminating at the February 1976 Party Congress: "Our Party is rendering and will render support to peoples who are fighting for their freedom -- we are acting as our revolutionary conscience and our communist convictions permit us."[10]

No account of Soviet action in the Third World can ignore the fierce rivalry between the USSR and her giant neighbor, Communist China. Competition in the Third World between the two senior Communist powers is knife edged. Relations between the Soviet Union and the People's Republic of China degenerated rapidly during the early 1960s, and reached such a pitch of hostility that a conflict erupted in the spring and summer of 1969. Sharp rivalry continued to be a feature of Sino-Soviet relations through the 1970s. As a leading authority on Soviet operations in Africa, Colin Legum concludes:

> The USSR loses no opportunity to try to diminish the influence of Western powers in the third world (especially in areas where it has strategic interests of its own); but its policies toward the third world show an even greater desire to undermine the position of the People's Republic of China than that of the West.[11]

During the late 1970s and early 1980s the Soviet Union became increasingly integrated into the world economy.[12] A succession of harvests marred by mismanagement and bad weather compelled the USSR to import very substantial quantities of grain and animal feed. Soviet ships deliver grain from Canada to meet Cuban needs. A massive fishing fleet has been developed to meet Russian requirements for protein.

Self-sufficient though the USSR may be in minerals, sheet mica and tantalum -- vital in electronic equipment -- must be imported. The Soviet Union must import more than half the bauxite she needs to make the key metal aluminum.[13] Some tin and tungsten must also be purchased abroad.

The Soviet Union has, for some years, been the leading oil producer of the world. Vast oil riches in Siberia are now being tapped. But wresting minerals from the Arctic reaches of Siberia is a difficult task indeed. They must then be shipped vast distances to the population and industrial centers in western Russia.

So oil problems loom on the horizon for the Soviets. Oil exports are a major source of hard currency earnings. In turn such currency has financed the purchase of advanced western technology. In this way the USSR has been able to meet the interest payments on its accumulated debts to western banks and governments. A decline in Soviet oil production would thus have serious consequences.

Moreover, the nations of eastern Europe have been utterly dependent on the Soviet Union for oil and many other critical minerals. Already the Russians are shipping oil bought in the Middle East to Eastern European refineries.

Thus the Soviet Union has been forced into the world market. Unfortunately, the USSR must find its critical minerals in precisely the same areas, Africa and the Middle East, that are so crucial to the United States, Western Europe, and Japan. A possibility of future conflict is thus foreshadowed.

Soviet actions spoke with even greater authority than Soviet words. Russian airborne forces were increased and their capabilities expanded. Tactical aviation was completely re-equipped, and transformed from a defensive fighter force to an arm capable of offensive and interdiction operations. Long range air transport was significantly improved and its capabilities demonstrated in major airlifts to Syria, to Angola, and to Ethiopia. The Soviet Navy grew apace.

Such instruments of Soviet policy found increasing employment in the 1970s, ranging far afield. A sampling of Russian operations will serve to illustrate the Kremlin's emergence upon the Third World stage.

In 1970 a protracted visit by the Soviet fleet helped sustain a regime in Somalia against an attempt at overthrow. To shield Guinea against Portuguese incursions, a Soviet naval West African patrol was established.

Nor was the air force idle. In 1970 Soviet fighter units were dispatched to Egypt, and engaged the Israeli Air Force in prolonged combat. During the October War of 1973 a massive airlift of weapons and equipment from the USSR to Syria was mounted.

But the most dramatic Russian operations in the Third World took place in Angola in 1975 and in the Ogaden War of 1978. Before intervening in Angola the Kremlin made sure that no U.S. opposition would be forthcoming. U.S. reaction was effectively hamstrung by the revulsion against foreign intervention engendered by the Vietnam experience. The airlift of substantial numbers of Cuban troops to Angola furnished ample proof of the emerging air transport capability of the Soviet Air Force.

In the Ogaden War Moscow turned a potentially disastrous situation to profit. A Soviet client state, Somalia, laid aggressive claim to territory in Ethiopian hands. The Russians abandoned Somalia and moved massively and swiftly to the aid of Ethiopia. Inasmuch as the Russians were defending the territorial integrity of Ethiopia against aggression, U.S. intervention was thoroughly frustrated. Thus was Moscow able to place itself on "the side of the angels" in this conflict. Against a tough foe the Soviets waged an effective campaign employing armor, helicopters, and fighter bombers.

Although the Kremlin lost the Somalian naval base of Berbera, the Russians not only succeeded, as Kenneth G. Weiss points out:

. . . in rescuing and embellishing their own
prestige in the Mideast and Africa, they dealt
a blow to U.S. international prestige. . . .
The U.S. response to Soviet involvement was
viewed by many as weak. . . . In peacetime the
perception of power is almost as important as
the reality of power.[16]

Shock waves reverberated throughout the world when
the Soviet Union occuped Afghanistan in December of
1979. The motives for this Kremlin action remain a
matter of conjecture and debate. Whether the
advantages to the USSR outweigh the disadvantages,
especially in the face of continued Afghan guerrilla
opposition, is a question for argument. The Soviet
action triggered a strong U.S. response, particularly
the formal activation of the Rapid Deployment Joint
Task Force.
Nonetheless, the invasion of Afghanistan was
eloquent testimony to the development of Soviet
military capabilities. As John Erickson states:

If Brezhnev had asked the general staff back
in 1973: 'Can you carry off such a campaign?'
the answer would have been no. Now the
general staff says, 'We can.'[17]

However the most salient feature of the Afghanistan
crisis may be that it is the first time, in the post
Second World War era, that the Kremlin has invaded and
occupied a nation other than a satellite state in
eastern Europe.
Whether the Soviet Union is engaged in a deliberate
strategy of waging a "resource war" against the west is
a hotly debated question. Certainly the Kremlin turned
a number of opportune situations and fortunate
circumstances to good account. It cannot be denied
that, whether by design or by good fortune, the Soviet
Union and its allies have established powerful
positions in Africa and the Middle East, areas whose
mineral riches are critical to the economies of the
United States, Western Europe, and Japan. Thus
ensconced in Africa and the Middle East the Kremlin
does pose a long term threat to the west.
At the end of 1981 approximately 69,000 troops from
the Soviet Union and her allies were deployed in a
number of Middle Eastern and African countries.[18] In
North Africa and the Middle East Soviet bloc forces are
to be found in Algeria, Libya, Syria, Iraq, and South
Yemen. Soldiers from the USSR and her partners are
stationed in Angola, the Congo, Ethiopia, Gabon,
Guinea, Mozambique, and Tanzania.
Libya occupies a particularly strategic position,
facing north to the narrows of the central

Mediterranean and south toward the nations across the Sahara. Soviet pilots fly MiG-25 reconnaissance planes and Tu-22 reconnaissance bombers from Libyan airbases.[19] Russian naval base facilities have been completed in Benghazi and Tripoli. A second major military airbase was brought into service in 1979 at Banbah. Eight new airfields are currently under construction.

Libya also serves as a massive storehouse of Soviet weaponry. The International Institute for Strategic Studies indicates that, in July of 1982, 2,900 main battle tanks were in Libyan hands, including Russian T-62s and T-72s and Italian built Leopard 1s.[20] Some 555 warplanes are to be found in the Libyan Air Force, with 175 MiG-23 interceptors, 72 MiG-21 fighters, and 46 French F-1 fighters in the front rank.[21]

Small in population, Libya possesses far more equipment than her meager forces can operate. Most of the tanks and many of the warplanes are consequently in storage. More than 6,000 Russian troops are committed to Libya to guard these stockpiles and assist the Libyan forces.[22] Pakistani, Palestinian, North Korean, and Yugoslav aircrew fly and maintain many of the warplanes in the so-called Libyan air force.[23] Pakistanis pilot the French built F-1s. A squadron of MiG-21s is flown by the North Koreans.

Libya is a main center for training terrorists and distributing arms to revolutionary movements all over the world. Cadres trained in Libya are especially active in Western Europe. Weapons flow from Libya to places as widely distant as Northern Ireland and the Philippines.

South Yemen is another key strategic area for Soviet interests in the Middle East and Southwest Asia. Here, 1500 Soviet troops are stationed, including a motorized rifle battalion.[24] Some 800 Cubans serve as advisors to Yemeni forces. Three hundred twenty five East German airmen fly and maintain 50 MiG-21 fighters. Soviet fliers operate 25 MiG-23 interceptors.

The main airbase at Aden has been improved and hardened shelters for fighters are under construction. Four supplementary airfields permit dispersed operations. The Aden airfield can handle 50 transport aircraft a day, a key staging base for the deployment of Soviet bloc forces into the area.

Naval facilities at Aden have been substantially upgraded during 1980-1981. Now Aden can sustain a squadron of five destroyers. Docks can unload five 10,000 ton freighters. Oil or water tankers of 30,000 tons can be handled at two berths.

Of greatest value to Moscow, however, is the comprehensive -- and continually expanding -- electronic complex established in Yemen. Electronic surveillance gleans information about activities in the

Indian Ocean and surrounding territories. Long range
communication equipment links Yemen with the Soviet
homeland.

Other Arab nations are not neglected by the Soviet
bloc. Russian, Cuban, and East German military
advisers and personnel are assigned to Algeria, Iraq,
and Syria. The Israelis have been astonished at the
large stocks of Soviet weaponry they have seized in the
Lebanon War of 1982, far more equipment than the
Palestine Liberation Organization could absorb and
operate.

Angola and Ethiopia play key roles in Soviet
strategy in Africa. In Angola, according to the
International Institute for Strategic Studies, 18,000
Cuban soldiers and 450 East German troops have been
stationed. East German strength in Africa fluctuates
with the exigencies of the crisis in Poland.

Thousands of Cuban experts have stepped into the
shoes of the Portuguese and are operating the
administrative and economic structure of Angola.[26]
Bulgarian, Czech, Romanian, and Russian civilian
technicians are also at work in Angola.

The major harbor at Luanda is being systematically
improved and could provide a base for Soviet warships
in the south Atlantic. Long range Russian Tu-95
aircraft fly patrol over the South Atlantic.

Soviet bloc forces in Angola are currently engaged
in active combat. They support the People's Republic
regime in Luanda agianst strong guerrilla opposition.
They train, arm, and support the South-West Africa
People's Organization in its guerrilla campaign in
neighboring Namibia. In retaliation, South African
Defense Forces, entrusted with maintaining stability in
Namibia, unleash powerful counter-blows deep into
Angola. Namibia is a rich prize, packed with diamonds,
copper, and uranium. It features one of the best
natural harbors on the west coast of Africa, Walvis
Bay.

In Ethiopia, Soviet bloc forces are the mainstay of
the military dictatorship of Colonel Mengistu.
According to French sources, as many as 20,000 Cuban
soldiers, 3,750 East German troops, and 3,500 Russian
military personnel have been stationed in Ethiopia.
One thousand South Yemeni troops and a fighter bomber
squadron also have served in Ethiopia. It should be
emphasized that Cuban troop strength fluctuates
dramatically as units are frequently rotated back and
forth from the island nation.

In defense of Ethiopia, Soviet bloc forces fought a
hard and fierce conflict, the Ogaden War, with Somalia
in 1977-1978. Combat operations have continued against
a potent insurgent movement and supporting Somali
troops in the keenly disputed area of Eritrea. On the
other hand, the Cubans are training, equipping, and

supporting guerrilla movements dedicated to the overthrow of the present governments of bordering Sudan and Kenya.

Important too are the naval facilities being developed at the ports of Assab and Massawa. East German engineers are especially active in the construction of these naval facilities.

Most significantly, the Russians are completing in the central highlands east of Addis Ababa a truly impressive array of comprehensive electronic installations. It is virtually impossible to "sneeze" in the Red Sea, Persian Gulf, or north Indian Ocean areas without Soviet knowledge of the fact.

The regimes of Libya, Ethiopia, and South Yemen are linked by treaty. A supreme council exists to facilitate joint diplomatic and military ventures. Thus has the Kremlin gained a powerful strategic position.

The USSR and its allies are active in other corners of Africa as well. In Mozambique Russian, Cuban, Czech, East German, and Romanian advisers and technicians are hard at work. The East Germans fly and maintain a force of MiG-21 interceptors. Maputo, one of the finest harbors on the east coast of the continent, commands the Mozambique Channel, a key "choke-point" where sea lanes converge to and from the Cape of Good Hope.

Clearly, the USSR depends very heavily upon its partners in its intervention strategy in Africa and the Middle East. Cuba, East Germany and other bloc countries contribute the overwhelming majority of forces committed to the Third World. Much has been written about this Soviet surrogate strategy employing so-called "proxy" forces. The advantages to the Soviet Union are obvious and substantial. But it would be a serious error to view bloc forces as mere puppets of the Kremlin. Cuban and East German commitments and sacrifices are quite heavy. Such commitments must serve Cuban and East German interests as well as Soviet. It would be accurate to say that the major Communist allies are partners whose interests run parallel and whose military capabilities are complementary.

Roger E. Kanet underlines the significant role of the German Democratic Republic:

All the East European states have been involved militarily in Sub-Saharan Africa, but the GDR has been by far the most active. African politicians have sought out the GDR's training of military and security personnel, which has been conducted both in Africa and in East Germany.[27]

East German advisers and troops are to be found in Algeria, Angola, Ethiopia, Libya, Mozambique, South Yemen, and Syria. East Germans serve as security guard contingents for Marxist-Leninist African governments, as well as furnishing key personnel for the secret police. Excellent East German fighter squadrons provide air defense in Angola, Mozambique, and South Yemen. GDR engineers and technicians are active in the construction of naval installations in Angola, Ethiopia, and Mozambique. Top East German leaders have traveled widely in Africa.[28] Erich Honecker, head of the GDR Socialist Unity Party, visited Angola, Zambia, Mozambique, and Ethiopia in 1979. The commander of the East German Army, General Heinz Hoffman, traveled twice in Africa, visiting Guinea, the Congo, Angola, Zambia, Mozambique, and Ethiopia.

Why is the GDR so deeply involved in Africa? The East German Communists have long been known for their rigid adherence to Marxist-Leninism, often viewing divergent developments in Czechoslovakia, Hungary, and Romania with a hostile eye. It is thus logical for the GDR to forge ideological links with the most radical African regimes.

In spite of its small population, the GDR is a formidable industrial nation. In the future the GDR may find markets in Africa for her manufactured goods. Although German engineering and technical skills have made the GDR an industrial power, she lacks virtually every natural resource except lignite and potash. In the future East Germany may need to rely much less on the USSR and much more on African sources for a wide range of needed raw materials.

Rivalry between the two German states, the GDR and the Federal Republic of Germany. has been very keen. East Germany has been at pains to win recognition in the world as a truly sovereign state. As Roger E. Kanet notes, "The continuing efforts of the GDR to strengthen its international and domestic position vis-a-vis West Germany have had a strong motivating force on the development of Berlin's relations with sub-Saharan Africa."[29]

However it is Cuba that is the mainstay of Soviet bloc operations in the Third World. Cuban military advisers and troops are to be found in Angola, Benin, the Congo, Ethiopia, Gabon, Guinea-Bissau, Mozambique, and Sierra Leone.[30] In the Middle East, Cuban advisers are assigned to South Yemen and Iraq. Cuban military personnel are at work in Grenada and Nicaragua. At least one-fifth of Havana's armed forces are posted abroad. Approximately 40,000 Cuban troops are committed in Africa.[31] In proportion to population, this would represent an American overseas deployment of almost one million soldiers.

On the whole, Cuban troops have proven to be well

trained and have fought fairly well. Cuba has
developed large, well trained, and ably led reserves.
Thus far the Cubans have suffered defeat only at the
hands of South African troops -- who are first class.
The Cubans do need to improve cooperation between their
air force squadrons and their ground army units. The
Cubans have displayed the distaste for anti-guerrilla
operations normally found in formally trained soldiery.

Many of the Cuban soldiers dispatched overseas are
black or mixed and hence much more welcome in Africa
than other races. The continuing war waged against
white dominated South Africa also wins black African
approbation. The Cuban involvement in Ethiopia was in
defense of recognized legitimate boundaries against a
clearly aggressive Somalia.

African approval has not been unanimous however.
Ghana, Senegal, Kenya and the Sudan have asked for the
withdrawal of Cuban forces from the continent. Havana
is entangled in a morass of regional rivalries and
ethnic conflicts in Eritrea.

The sheer scale of Cuban commitment in Africa is
convincing proof of the sweep of Cuba's ambitious goals
in that continent. Anti-imperialism is the sharp edge
of Cuban ideology. As a Third World nation, Cuba feels
a strong sense of common cause with new countries
emerging from the ruins of old empires.

But the Cuban venture should not be viewed entirely
in the light of an anti-imperialist crusade. A variety
of motives are at work. The flamboyant Fidel Castro
has long cut a dashing figure on the world stage and
has sought a leadership role in the Third World. A
sense of community with black Africa is deeply felt.

The long term intent of Cuban policy is indicated
by the many civilian experts working in Africa and by
the education of African youth in Cuba.[32] Some 10,000
Cuban administrators, technicians, physicians, nurses,
and teachers serve in Africa. The best trained experts
have been committed in Africa. Eight thousand African
children a year attend special elementary and secondary
schools in Cuba under scholarship. Most of these
children come from Angola, Ethiopia, and Mozambique and
spend three to six years in Cuban schools.

Thus far the objectives pursued by Cuba and the
USSR in Africa and the Middle East permit the two
powers to work in close cooperation. In the future the
interests of the two nations may diverge, however, and
the United States should be alert to the opportunities
thus presented.

The Soviet Union and its partners have thus seized
upon opportune situations in the Third World, only
moving to intervene where circumstances have been
favorable. They have, for the most part, fought "on
the side of the angels" in defense of client regimes
against aggression.

The USSR and its allies have exploited regional antipathies to the hilt. In the Middle East Moscow has played upon Arab hostility toward Israel and the United States. Saudi Arabia, for instance, is much more concerned about Israeli and Iranian behavior than it is about Soviet. In Africa the Soviet bloc profited immensely from the death throes of the Portuguese Empire. Now an appropriate "villain" has been found in the South African regime and its "imperialist" backers. A number of the hyper-nationalistic African governments view South Africa as the major threat, and the Soviet bloc is seen as a welcome counterbalance.

It is important to note that Soviet intervention in the developing countries has been undertaken with great caution and deliberation. In Angola Moscow initially attempted to negotiate an end to the civil war. Both the USSR and Cuba assiduously sought to mediate the conflict between Ethiopia and Somalia. Escalation of intervention has been a step by step process in which the regional political and wider diplomatic settings have been thoroughly reconnoitered.

1. Watson, p. 2.

2. Bradford Dismukes and James M. McConnell, editors, Soviet Naval Diplomacy (New York, New York: Pergamon Press, 1979), p. 5.

3. Watson, p. 3.

4. Dismukes and McConnell, pp. 23-28.

5. Ibid., p. 26

6. Charles C. Petersen, Third World Military Elites In Soviet Perspective (Alexandria, Virginia: Center For Naval Analyses, November 1979), p. 37.

7. William J. Durch, The Cuban Military In Africa And The Middle East: From Algeria to Angola (Alexandria, Virginia: Center For Naval Analyses, September 1977), p. 1.

8. V.M. Kulish et. al., Military Force and International Relations (Arlington, Virginia: Joint Publications Research Service, 8 May 1973), p. 103.

9. Jacobsen, p. 17.

10. Ibid.

11. Colin Legum, "Angola and the Horn of Africa," in Stephen S. Kaplan, ed., Diplomacy of Power (Washington, D.C.: The Brookings Institution), p. 573.

12. Dunn, pp. 20-22.

13. Clarence A. Robinson, Jr., "Defense Science Board Urges Multiyear Contracts," Aviation Week & Space Technology, 1 December 1980, p. 132.

14. Dunn, pp. 21-22.

15. See Legum for an excellent discussion of Soviet operations in Angola and the Horn of Africa.

16. Kenneth G. Weiss, The Soviet Involvement In The Ogaden War (Alexandria, Virginia: Center For Naval Analyses, February 1980), p. 36.

17. "Moscow's Military Machine," Time, 23 June 1980, p. 31.

18. Soviets Focus on Control Of Oil Flow From Region," Aviation Week & Space Technology, 14 December 1981, pp. 48-49.

19.   Youssef Bodansky, "Soviet Military Presence in Libya," Armed Forces Journal International, November 1980, p. 90.

20.   The International Institute for Strategic Studies, The Military Balance 1982-1983, p. 59.

21.   Ibid.

22.   Bodansky, p. 90.

23.   Ibid., pp. 90-91.

24.   The International Institute for Strategic Studies, The Military Balance 1982-1983, p. 59.

25.   Ibid., p. 66.

26.   George Volsky, "Cuba", Thomas H. Henriksen, ed., Communist Powers and Sub-Saharan Africa (Stanford, California: Hoover Institution Press, 1981), pp. 75-76.

27.   Roger E. Kanet, "East European States," in Henriksen, pp. 45-46.

28.   Ibid., p. 41.

29.   Ibid., p. 47.

30.   Volsky, in Henriksen, p. 74.

31.   Ibid., p. 75.

32.   Ibid.

IV
Instruments of Soviet Intervention: Tactical Airpower, Transport Aviation, and Airborne Forces

A massive and thorough expansion and modernization of Soviet tactical airpower got underway in the early 1970s. More than 1,000 fighters have emerged from Soviet factories each year from 1972 through 1980, more than twice the fighter production rate of the United States.[1] Fighter production in the USSR is now 1,300 a year.[2] The Soviet Union now possesses the largest tactical air force in the world, 4,480 combat aircraft and 2,300 armed helicopters.[3]

Moreover a generation of new warplanes now equips Soviet tactical aviation. The new aircraft boast twice the payload and range of the machines they supplant. Far more effective armament is now featured; new machine cannon, air to air missiles, and air to surface rockets. Above all, electronics are vastly improved. Doppler navigation systems, multi-mode attack radar, terrain avoidance radar, laser target designators, electro-optical attack systems, and electronic counter-measures suites are now standard equipment in warplanes in Soviet service. By 1981 such new models accounted for all air superiority fighters and three-quarters of ground support fighter bombers in the Soviet tactical air inventory.[4]

It must be emphasized that Russian warplanes exported abroad, even to allies, are "stripped-down" versions, bereft of advanced avionics, electronic systems, and armament. The Israeli triumph in the Lebanon War of 1982 must not lead the west into complacency. As Anthony H. Cordesman incisively notes:

> In short, the West has no massive technical superiority that can give it the 80:1 kill ratios Israel has achieved over Syria. Israel's advantage comes from superior tactics and training, and from ruthless and consistent Soviet denial of the advanced military technology the Arabs need to compete.[5]

A complete account of all Russian tactical warplanes lies beyond the scope of this study. The focus will be upon those aircraft most widely deployed abroad and most relevant in supporting Soviet intervention in the developing countries.

A mainstay of Soviet bloc operations in Africa is the MiG-21 fighter. An older vintage design, the MiG-21 continues to be manufactured in better armed and more sophisticated variants. Some 730 MiG-21s are in service with Russian squadrons.[6] Equipped with a variety of avionic and electronic installations, the MiG-21bis is a genuine multi-role and all weather warplane. A single seat, single engine fighter, the MiG-21 is agile, very stable in low speed handling, and reliable. In the air superiority mode, the MiG-21bis is equipped with a twin barrel 23mm. machine cannon and four infra-red homing missiles of the improved AA-8 type.[7] Standard payload for ground attack missions is either four 550 lb. bombs or two AS-7 radio command guided missiles.

Combat radius of the MiG-21 is limited, from 342 to 559 miles, depending on mission.[8] Vision to the rear from the cockpit requires a rear view mirror, a serious handicap in dogfighting. The MiG-21 is no match for the new generation of western fighters, the U.S F-14, F-15, F-16 and the French F-1 and Mirage 2000. But in the hands of a skilled pilot the MiG-21 could give a good account of itself against a machine of its own generation such as a Northrop F-5E or a Mirage III.

Far more significant are the MiG-23G, an all weather air superiority and interception fighter, and the MiG-27J, an all weather ground attack and long range strike warplane. These variable geometry machines are now the standard Soviet combat fighters. The MiG-23G is armed with a twin barrel 23mm. machine cannon and six air to air missiles; four AA-7 semi-active radar homing, with a range of 32 1/2 kilometers, and two AA-8 infra-red homing, all-aspect rockets for close-in air combat.[9] Combat radius is substantial, 746 miles.

The MiG-23G is clearly the equal, if not the superior, of the widely used F-4 Phantom. It is inferior, however to the F-14, F-15 and Mirage 2000. In dogfighting it is an easy victim for an F-16. But the MiG-23 can unleash AA-7 missiles at a range that the Sidewinder rockets employed by the F-16 cannot reach. In July 1982, 2075 MiG-23s were operational with Frontal Aviation and Air Defense.[10]

Designed for low level attack, the MiG-27J features a Doppler navigation system, terrain avoidance radar, a laser target designator, and other electro-optical systems. Armed with a six barrel 23mm machine cannon, the MiG-27 can carry a maximum payload of 7,718 lb., and operating radius is 342 to 497 miles. Usually,

four 1,110 lb. bombs or AS-10 semi-active laser guided
missiles are carried. A new air to surface rocket, the
AS-14, is being introduced. In July 1982, 550 MiG-27s
were in service with Russian tactical aviation.[12]
 Capable of operating in all weather conditions, the
MiG-27 is a formidable ground attack machine.
Optimized for low level penetration it is a potent
threat to such rear area targets as airbases.
 Strike warplanes, however, must be able to absorb
considerable damage from anti-aircraft fire, and twin
engines are deemed essential in such aircraft. An
imposing workload falls upon the single crew member of
the MiG-27, who must pilot, navigate, and operate all
weapons systems. The MiG-27 lacks a system for
refueling in air, a singular limitation upon its
operating range.
 A new generation of Russian tactical warplanes is
now coming into service. In 1982 the first units of a
new ground attack machine, the Sukhoi Su-25, saw action
in Afghanistan. Armed with a Gatling type heavy
machine cannon, the Su-25 carries a heavy payload of
10,000 lbs.[13] A twin engine machine, the Su-25
features a range of some 650 nautical miles.
 In 1985 a Soviet fighter, the MiG-29, designed
specifically for the air superiority role, is expected
to enter service. Twin engines will endow the new
fighter with a thrust to weight ratio of 1.3 to 1.4,
affording high acceleration and the ability to operate
with minimum use of afterburner.[14] A raised cockpit
design ensures excellent visibility in all directions.
A new radar, featuring a "look-down", "shoot-down"
capability and a 45 nautical mile target tracking
range, equips the new fighter.[15] The MiG-29 will be
armed with six air to air missiles, including the new
AA-9, a semi-active radar seeking rocket able to
intercept a target as small as one meter^2 at a range of
17 1/2 kilometers.[16] Introduction of the MiG-29 and
other new fighters into service will give the USSR the
ability to fight on equal terms with the F-15, F-16,
F-18, and Mirage 2000.
 Above all, the USSR will deploy, in 1983, airborne
warning and control aircraft. Such aircraft proved a
key element in the Lebanon War of 1982. A version of
the Ilyushin Il-76 will be employed by the Soviet
Union.
 The 1970s saw a tremendous expansion of Soviet
helicopters in military service. By July 1982 more
than 3,450 helicopters of all types were operational.[17]
The Russians have concentrated on developing their
armed helicopter capability. More than 2,300 armed
helicopters are now in service, exceeding the number of
U.S. Cobras, and attack helicopters are delivered from
Soviet factories at a rate of 15 per month.[18] In
Soviet military organization helicopters are viewed as

tactical warplanes and hence constitute an integral part of Frontal Aviation.

The key attack helo in Soviet service is the Miliutin Mi-24 Hind, more than 1,000 of which are operational. A twin engine machine with a crew of two, the Hind can attain a top speed of 204 miles per hour and features a cruising range of 372 miles.[19] Heavily armed, the most advanced version, the Mi-24E, is equipped with a turret mounted four barrel 12.7mm. machine gun. Pylons on the stub wings can carry 128 57mm. rockets plus four 550 lb. bombs or four AT-6 Spiral anti-tank missiles.[20] The AT-6 is radio command guided and has a range estimated at 5,000 meters.

Extensive measures have been taken to ensure survivability in the Hind. Engine exhausts are cooled to reduce infra-red emmision. Intake plugs and sand filters protect the engines. The windshield is made of armor glass. Titanium alloy armor plate shields the underside of the fuselage and the front of the gunner's cockpit.

A formidable attack machine, the Mi-24 is heavily employed in combat in Afghanistan and Ethiopia. Maneuvers clearly indicate that the Russians regard the attack "chopper" as an integral and very important member of the combined arms team.

Military Transport Aviation has been greatly developed by the USSR in the 1970s and massively employed in the Middle East, Angola, Ethiopia, and Afghanistan. In July of 1982 VTA numbered 605 transports, including 55 giant Antonov An-22s, 150 Ilyushin Il-76 turbofan transports, and 400 Antonov An-12 turboprop machines.[21] To be sure U.S. airlift enjoys an advantage in very long range operations and in sheer tonnage capability. Much more serious a handicap, however, is the lack of refueling in air for Soviet transports.

But the USSR is steadily expanding its airlift capacity, adding 36 Il-76 transports each year. At present VTA can carry one airborne division, with all its equipment and supplies for three days, 1,000 miles.[22] Or the combat elements of two airborne divisions can be projected the same distance. The Soviet Civil Air Fleet, which employs the same transports as VTA, can augment airlift by one airborne division or two motorized rifle divisions.[23]

Moreover, Russian transports are designed to fly from unpaved strips, operate in primitive conditions, and are equipped with gear for loading and unloading cargo.[24] Ironically, such requirements are needed to operate within the USSR. But such capabilities are ideal for functioning in the Third World as well.

Transport undercarriage is very rugged, frequently multi-wheel, and tire pressure can be adjusted to terrain. Motors are started by onboard auxiliary turbines. Either pressure or gravity refueling can be employed.

Overhead trolley hoists are fitted and also serve as winches for handling cargo. In the floor are rails for chain conveyors. Cargo can thus be handled directly to trucks.

Maintenance requirements are deliberately kept simple. Indeed the Il-76 can carry a set of tools, spare parts, a mechanic and electrician. Thus outfitted the Il-76 can be kept operational for more than 90 days.

The workhorse of VTA is a four engine turboprop, the Antonov 12PB. One hundred soldiers or 22 tons of cargo can be carried 2,236 miles by the An-12PB.[25]

Far more significant is the Ilyushin 76T, a four engine turbofan with sufficient excess power to make short take off and landing possible from rough airstrips. The Il-76T can carry 44 tons of freight 3,100 miles in approximately six hours.[26] It is large enough to transport any armored vehicle in Soviet service. Fitted for all weather and night operations, the Il-76T possesses a computer for flight control and landing approaches.

Aeroflot, the so-called commercial airline, is in reality a ready reserve for the VTA, commanded by an Air Force Marshal and manned by personnel with military training and experience.[27] Some 36 of the huge An-22s and 150 An-12s are flown by Aeroflot.[28] More than 100 new Il-76 transports have expanded Aeroflot troop capacity by 45 percent.

Aeroflot is employed regularly in the annual rotation of troops between the USSR and East Germany. Cuban troops were ferried to Angola by the VTA and Aeroflot. Aeroflot again augmented the VTA airlift of Russian and Cuban forces and equipment to Ethiopia. Regular routes are flown by Aeroflot, despite a clear financial loss, to the most remote corners of Africa. Aeroflot crews are thus very familiar with the terrain, conditions, and weather of the vital continent.

Eight airborne divisions, the largest airborne force in the world, constitute the most swiftly deployable Soviet forces.[29] Seven of the formations are at full strength and readiness. Another unit serves as a training cadre. Russian airborne troops number 55,000 and can be expanded by 100,000 reserves with recent training.[30] The special role of the Soviet airborne force is underlined by the fact that it is directly responsible to the Ministry of Defense. Russian airborne units have seen action from Czechoslovakia to Afghanistan. Currently, one division is stationed in the Soviet Far East and a brigade has been deployed to Tan Son Nhut in Vietnam.

A Soviet airborne division numbers approximately 7,900 men and includes three infantry regiments, an artillery regiment, and an assault gun battalion, an anti-aircraft battalion, and other supporting units.[31]

Artillery includes 18 of the versatile and easily handled D-30 122mm. howitzers. Eighteen RPU-14 multiple rocket launchers are also standard equipment, each unit capable of firing 16 round salvoes of 140mm. rockets. Heavy 120mm. mortars are divided among the infantry regiments, six to each unit. A Soviet airborne formation is thus backed by substantial firepower.[32]

Anti-tank capabilities are also respectable.[33] Eighteen armored vehicles armed with 85mm. guns and 9 armored cars firing guided missiles provide a mobile anti-tank defense. They are augmented by 12 85mm. guns, 42 AT-4 guided missile launchers, and 144 APG-9 73mm. recoilless guns.

Anti-aircraft protection is not inconsiderable either. Thirty-six 23mm. guns and 132 SA-7 anti-aircraft missiles are divided among the infantry contingents.

One infantry regiment in each division is a mechanized infantry formation, equipped with 107 BMD combat vehicles and 12 armored cars.[34] Three such units can be gathered together, creating in effect an air portable "mini" motor rifle division.

The BMD is a compact, fully tracked, amphibious, armored vehicle that is air dropped by multiple parachute and retro-rocket.[35] It carries a crew of two and five infantrymen. The turret of the BMD carries a 73mm. smoothbore, low velocity cannon, a light machine gun, and an anti-tank guided missile launcher. More recent versions feature a new turret with a 30mm. high velocity cannon. Armor protection has also been improved in the new models. The BMD has a top speed of 42 miles per hour and a cruising range of 192 miles.

The BMD presents a particular challenge to U.S. paratroop and airmobile contingents, which lack a suitably armed counterpart. French Panhard armored cars and British Scorpion light tanks furnish French and British light forces with well armed counters to the BMD.

The combination of Soviet air transport and allied troops is the key card the Kremlin has chosen to play. The Soviet airborne force supported by attack helicopters is another strong card that Moscow may bring into play in Africa or the Middle East.

1.   Clarence A. Robinson, Jr., "Soviet Union Defensive Buildup Detailed by Weinberger," <u>Aviation Week & Space Technology</u>, 5 October 1981, p. 18.

2.   U. S. Department of Defense, <u>Soviet Military Power</u>, (Washington, D. C.: U.S. Government Printing Office, [September, 1981]), p. 12.

3.   The International Institute for Strategic Studies, <u>The Military Balance 1982-1983</u>, p. 16.

4.   Robinson, p. 19.

5.   Anthony H. Cordesman, "The Sixth Arab-Israeli Conflict: Military lessons for American Defense Planning," <u>Armed Forces Journal International</u>, August 1982, p. 30.

6.   The International Institute for Strategic Studies, <u>The Military Balance 1982-1983</u>, pp. 16-17.

7.   Bill Gunston, Consultant Editor, <u>The Encyclopedia of World Airpower</u>, (New York, New York: Crescent Books, 1980), p. 264.

8.   Robinson.

9.   Ibid. See also Georg Panyalev, "The Ram-L Air Superiority Fighter," <u>International Defense Review</u>, December 1981, pp. 1609, 1612.

10.   The International Institute for Strategic Studies, <u>The Military Balance 1982-1983</u>, p. 14, 16.

11.   Robinson.

12.   The International Institute for Strategic Studies, <u>The Military Balance 1982-1983</u>, p. 16.

13.   Soviets Test Attack Aircraft in Afghanistan," <u>Aviation Week & Space Technology</u>, 7 June 1982, pp. 54-56.

14.   Panyalev, pp. 1611-1612.

15.   "Soviets Deploy Updated MiG-25 Foxbat Fighter," <u>Aviation Week & Space Technology</u>, 7 June 1982, pp. 54-56.

16.   Panyalev, p. 1612.

17.   The International Institute for Strategic Studies, <u>The Military Balance 1982-1983</u>, p. 17.

42

18.   Deborah G. Meyer, p. 42.

19.   Nikolai Cherikov, "The Soviet Mi-24 Hind Attack Helicopter," International Defense Review, September 1981, p. 1133.

20.   Ibid.

21.   The International Institute for Strategic Studies, The Military Balance 1982-1983.

22.   Collins, p. 276.

23.   Ralph Ostrich, "Aeroflot," Armed Forces Journal International, May 1981, p. 45.

24.   Peter Borgart, "The Soviet Transport Air Force: aircraft and capabilities," International Defense Review, June 1979, p. 945.

25.   John W.R. Taylor, "Gallery Of Soviet Aerospace Weapons," Air Force Magazine, March 1981, p. 108.

26.   Deborah M. Kyle, "Russia's Il-76 Transport: Ten Years Ahead of C-X?" Armed Forces Journal International, July 1980, p. 18.

27.   Ostrich. p. 42.

28.   James H. Hansen, "Soviet Projection Forces -- Their Status and Outlook," Armed Forces Journal International, October 1981, p. 82.

29.   The International Institute for Strategic Studies, The Military Balance 1982-1983, p. 14.

30.   "Soviets Improving Force Mobility," Aviation Week & Space Technology, 21 December 1981, p. 57.

31.   U.S. Army Armor Center, Organization and Equipment of the Soviet Army, (Fort Knox, Kentucky: U.S. Army Armor Center, 1981), pp. 2-15.

32.   Ibid.

33.   Ibid.

34.   Ibid., pp. 2-17.

35.   Ibid., pp. 5-48.

V
Instruments of Soviet Intervention: The Navy and Merchant Fleet

A formidable Soviet fleet has emerged in the course of the 1970s and 1980s. In January, 1982 the Russian Navy included 3 VTOL aircraft carriers, 2 helicopter carriers, 26 guided missile cruisers, 42 guided missile destroyers, 32 large frigates, and 86 amphibious warfare ships.[1] The array of submarines in Soviet service numbered 67 cruise missile attack (48 of them nuclear fueled) and 136 first class attack units (61 of them nuclear fueled).[2] Another 90 ballistic missile firing submarines serve in the strategic role.

A tremendous naval building program proceeds apace. Twelve large warships are currently under construction in addition to large carriers and small frigates.[3] Five major yards build some ten new submarines each year, eight of them nuclear fueled.[4] Nor are supporting units neglected. Two 80,000 ton floating drydocks have been purchased from Japan and Sweden and service the Northern Fleet at Murmansk and the Pacific Fleet at Vladivostok. Two modern hospital ships, built in Poland, are stationed with the Black Sea Fleet and the Pacific Fleet. The long range impact of Soviet naval expansion is incisively summarized by Michael MccGwire:

> . . . every three years the Soviet navy will acquire a powerful new battle group comprising a heavily armed battlecruiser, 3 cruisers and about 10 large destroyers. The first three or four of these battle groups will rely on a Kiev to provide a modicum of sea-based air support, but thereafter we might expect to see one fully capable air-superiority carrier for every two battle groups.[5]

Operations far distant from home waters have vastly increased for the Russian fleet. Out of home area deployments grew from 35,300 ship days in 1969 to 57,800 ship days in 1980.[6] The Atlantic Ocean and the

43

Mediterranean Sea still claim the most Soviet naval attention. But the most dramatic increases in deployment of the Russian fleet have been to the Pacific and Indian Oceans. The composition of naval units deployed far from home base areas reflects a fundamental change in Soviet fleet missions. Surface warships now account for a considerably greater share in operations and auxiliary ships play a sharply increased role. As Charles Petersen points out:

> Oceangoing surface warships -- the premier instruments of naval diplomacy -- have rapidly risen to prominence in the Soviet Navy's forward deployments. . . . Improvements in Soviet seamanship and in the complexity and sophistication of Soviet tactics have been roughly commensurate.[7]

Increased numbers of ships and expanded operations are only part of the developing Soviet fleet. New Russian warships are large, with weapons mounted in the ship and with ample space for ammunition and fuel. Such warships are designed and equipped for long range operations and sustained combat. Soviet units are furnished with redundant combat systems and alternative operating modes which ensure a high degree of reliability and survivability.[8]

Three VTOL aircraft carriers of the Kiev class are in service and a fourth is nearing completion. Weighing 44,000 tons at full load, the Kiev can make 32 knots and has a cruising range of 13,500 nautical miles at 18 knots.[9]

Four twin launchers can fire surface to surface missiles with a range of 300 nautical miles. A total of 24 surface to surface missiles are carried. Anti-aircraft defense is provided by four twin rocket launchers augmented by four 76.2mm. cannon and eight 30mm. six barrel machine cannon. Weapons against submarines include a twin rocket launcher, ten torpedo tubes, and, of course, the helicopters based on the carrier.

The air contingent on this Tactical Aircraft Carrying Cruiser, as the Russians designate the Kiev, usually consists of 20 Kamov-25 helicopters and 15 Yakovlev-36MP vertical take off and landing fighters.[10] The "A" version of the Ka-25 is equipped with dipping sonar, sonobuoys, torpedoes and depth charges for antisubmarine warfare. Long range surface to surface missile targeting is the task entrusted to the "B" variant of the Kamov helicopter. Thus far the Yak-36 has operated in air defense and antiship missions. Constricted by the VTOL mode of operation, range and payload of the Yak-36 are sharply limited.

The Kiev class warship represents a compromise

between a guided missile cruiser and an aircraft carrier. It does provide a modest degree of air support at sea. But the Russians have yet to develop a V/STOL warplane comparable to the British Sea Harrier. From the standpoint of a genuine carrier capability, the compromise embodied in the Kiev leaves much to be desired.

Far more impressive is the new battle cruiser, the Kirov. One of these new Missile Cruisers, as the Russians officially term them, is now operational and a second is building in a Leningrad shipyard. Weighing an estimated 23,400 tons at full load, the Kirov features a combined nuclear and oil fueled steam propulsion system which makes possible a top speed of 34 knots and virtually unlimited range.[11] A long and wide ship, the Kirov also possesses one more deck than U.S. warships affording very large internal volume.

Armament features 20 surface to surface missiles, with a 300 nautical mile range, mounted in inclined launching tubes.[12] Kirov is shielded from air attack by twelve vertical launchers for long range anti-aircraft rockets and two twin missile launchers for short range defense. Two 100mm. cannon and eight 30mm. six barrel machine cannon provide further defense against enemy warplanes. Antisubmarine weaponry includes a twin, reloadable, launcher that unleashes a cruise missile with a homing torpedo and eight torpedo tubes. An estimated three to five Ka-25 helicopters can operate from the stern landing deck. A large variable depth sonar is carried by the Kirov in addition to a very powerful low frequency bow mounted sonar.

Electronic equipment of the Kirov is elaborate, complex, and sophisticated. Noteworthy are the long range high frequency equipment and satellite communications systems. At least 16 radar systems can be identified. Some 24 electronic countermeasures systems are on board. Moreover as Captain J.W. Kehoe and K.S. Brower emphasize:

> Analysis of the Kirov's sensors indicates that the ship's designers . . . paid particular attention to minimizing the problems of electromagnetic incompatibility and interference. Particularly evident is the shielding of cables and waveguides, physical isolation of electronic systems and judicious antenna siting.[13]

The Kirov is indeed a formidable and versatile warship.

The USSR is also building a new class of 12,000 ton cruisers in Black Sea shipyards. Three of these ships are currently under construction, eight in all are expected to enter service with the fleet. Powered by gas turbine engines, they promise to be fast units and feature the usual comprehensive array of weaponry.

A new class of general purpose destroyer, the Sovremennyy, is appearing in the ranks of Soviet warships. Two are now in service and two more are building. A considerable number are anticipated in the class. Conventional steam machinery gives the 7,800 ton destroyer a maximum speed of 34 knots.[15]

Configured for shore bombardment and antiship missions, the Sovremennyy features four fully automatic 130mm. cannon and eight surface to surface missile launchers. Two rocket launchers and four 30mm. six barrel machine cannon serve for anti-aircraft purposes. Antisubmarine defense is minimal, a close range multiple rocket launcher and four tubes for homing torpedoes. A Ka-25B is also carried. The Sovremennyy should prove to be a very effective replacement for the older Skoryy class destroyers.

Another new large destroyer class, the Udaloy, is particularly well suited to be an ASW escort for a carrier battle group. Formally designated as a Large Antisubmarine Ship, the 8,200 ton Udaloy features two quadruple launchers for ASW cruise missiles, eight torpedo tubes, and two of the new Ka-32 helicopters.[16] Anti-aircraft protection features eight missile launchers of a new type, two 100mm. guns, and four 30mm. Gatling machine cannon. A large variable depth sonar and bow mounted sonar equip Udaloy. Two of the class are operational and four more are building.

The new large warships of the USSR clearly reflect the demands of operations far distant from the homeland. A Kiev and Kirov escorted by Udaloys and Sovremennyys will make an impressive and effective battle group for intervention in African waters or the Indian Ocean.

The most lethal threat to vital sealanes in time of war is the Russian submarine armada. It is most unlikely that submarines would be unleashed short of a global conflagration. In a total war situation many Soviet attack submarines would be dedicated to the defense of Russian ballistic missile submarines held in strategic reserve. Others would seek to destroy U.S. super carriers. However operations against sealanes do rank no less than second in the array of Soviet wartime missions.[17] The sharply increasing dependence of western economies upon seaborne imports make sealanes ever more inviting and vulnerable targets. In wartime submarines, operating as a team with satellite surveillance systems and long range warplanes armed with air to surface missiles, could well prove decisive weapons against the super carrier. And unleashed upon the sealanes submarines could wreak havoc upon U.S. and other western troops and supplies being shipped to critical arenas overseas.

In peacetime the submarine is much less useful. The very nature of the undersea predator does not lend itself to the visible aspects of naval diplomacy. In peacetime surface fleet confrontations, however, account must always be taken of the inevitable presence of the menace lurking in the deep.

Representative of Soviet cruise missile firing submarines is the nuclear fueled Charlie class. Weighing 5,100 tons, Charlie II is capable of 26 knots underwater and is armed with six torpedo tubes and eight missile launchers.[18] The SS-9 can be launched submerged, carries either a high explosive or nuclear warhead, and can range out to 60 miles with the assistance of aerial guidance.[19] Seventeen Charlies are in service and more are building.

Typical of the nuclear fueled attack craft is the Victor class, 31 of which are operational and more under construction. Possessing a good turn of speed at 29 knots, the Victor III carries eight tubes which can unleash torpedoes or an antisubmarine missile with a range of 50 nautical miles.[20]

Most spectacular of all is the Alfa, the swiftest and deepest diving submarine in the world. Constructed of titanium alloy, the nuclear fueled Alfa features a speed of 45 knots and can dive below 900 meters.[21] Highly automated, the Alfa requires only 45 crew members. Six tubes fire torpedoes or launch ASW missiles.

Alfa is cause for much concern on the part of U.S. and Allied fleets. Five Alfas are operational and ten more are under construction.

Diesel-electric submarines have not been neglected by the USSR. Such underwater craft offer many advantages, they are quiet, operate effectively in shallow waters, and are relatively inexpensive. Sixty Foxtrot class diesel submarines are in service. Armed with ten torpedo tubes, they have a range of 11,000 nautical miles.[22] The new Tango class are similarly armed but larger and faster, 14 are operational and more are building.

Naval Infantry in Soviet service is a small, 20,000 to 30,000 man force, in no way comparable to the U.S. Marine Corps in size or capabilities. It cannot carry out an assault landing against major opposition. But it is an elite force configured for a variety of specialized missions. In particular they are trained to seize such strategic areas as northern Norway in wartime. However, Soviet amphibious ships and personnel have been extremely active in the West African, Angolan, and Ethiopian operations, carrying supplies and Cuban troops.

Naval Infantry are organized in five regiments, two of which are stationed with the Pacific Fleet.[23] They deploy and maneuver regularly in the Mediterranean Sea, the Indian Ocean, and off the west coast of Africa. Unlike the American and British Marines, the Soviet Naval Infantry are highly mechanized and include a tank battalion, with a company of medium tanks, in each regiment. A transport helicopter company is also an integral component of each regiment for combined operations.

In addition to the usual array of specialized amphibious landing ships, the Soviet fleet possesses the world's largest force of military air cushion vehicles. No less than 50 such hovercraft are in service. The Aist class ACVs can each carry 220 soldiers and four light tanks at a speed of 65 knots.[24] ACVs are particularly valuable for operations along coastlines with shallow waters. Such areas include much of the Indian Ocean littoral, especially the Arabian peninsula.

Far more significant is the rapidly increasing role of the Soviet Naval Air Force. Russian naval air is overwhelmingly land based but is tightly integrated into fleet operations. In July of 1982 AVMF numbered 755 combat aircraft and 300 helicopters.[25]

Lacking a substantial carrier capability, maritime reconnaissance is an important function of long range naval aircraft. The four engine turboprop Tupolev-95D, with a maximum range of 11,000 miles, has proven especially useful in this role. The sleek and supersonic jet Tupolev-22, capable of a 4,000 mile subsonic cruising range, is much employed for electronic intelligence gathering and reconnaissance.

Carrier based aviation is very limited, some 40 Yak-36MPs.[26] The Yak-36 is a complex machine, employing supplementary engines to augment lift needed for vertical take off and landing. Short take off and landing is apparently precluded by stability and safety considerations. Armament, payload, and range are thus necessarily quite limited.[27] Electronic and avionic systems are rudimentary, limiting the machine to clear weather operations. It is estimated that the Yak fighter, armed with two AA-8 infra-red homing air to air missiles, can patrol for about an hour some 100 nautical miles from its carrier.[28] Equipped with a 23mm. machine cannon pod and carrying one ton of bombs the warplane can fly an attack mission over 200 nautical miles.

Construction of a nuclear fueled super carrier has been reported for some years.[29] Soviet planes have been observed practicing short landings with arresting gear on simulated carrier "decks" at land airbases. When the first true Soviet carrier will materialize remains to be seen.

Far more menacing are the land based AVMF bombers and strike warplanes. Most numerous, in July 1982, were 240 Tupolev-16C/G medium bombers.[30] An older plane, the Tu-16 is now being updated with the AS-6 Kingfish air to surface missile. Although slow, the Tu-16 possesses a radius of 2,000 miles.

Soviet Naval Aviation bombers are equipped for refueling in air, thus considerably augmenting operating radii. Another 70 Tu-16s serve in the tanker role.

Most formidable of all is the Tupolev-26, a strike bomber featuring powerful twin turbofan engines and a semi-variable geometry wing. Able to achieve 1,320 miles per hour at altitude, the Tu-26 has an estimated combat radius, unrefueled, of 2,485 miles.[31] Two hundred Tu-26s were operational in August 1982, divided between the Long Range Air Force and Naval Aviation.[32]

Main armament for Tu-16 and Tu-26 is the AS-6 Kingfish air to surface missile. The Kingfish can be launched 380 miles from its target.[33] Mid-course guidance must be provided by another aircraft or surface ship. Active radar guidance then homes the rocket onto its quarry at a speed of Mach 3.5. Designed specifically for the Tu-26, a new cruise missile with a range of 745 miles is expected to enter service in 1983.[34]

Teamed with submarines the Tu-26 represents the most lethal threat to U.S. and allied navies. Indeed, as Clarence A. Robinson, Jr. points out, the U.S. Navy

> . . . recently determined that the F-14 in the fleet air defense role with major improvements is the only fighter that can effectively counter the Tu-26 Backfire armed with increased-range, nuclear-armed air-to-surface cruise missiles.[35]

An analysis of the Soviet Navy must take into account the indispensable contributions of the Russian merchant fleet. Like Aeroflot, the merchant marine of the USSR is an armed forces auxiliary, tightly integrated into the operations of the Russian navy.

Soviet merchant shipping has grown very rapidly over the course of the last thirty years. In 1980 the Russian merchant fleet, some 18,600,000 deadweight tons, ranked ninth in the world in tonnage and fifth in numbers of ships.[36] Moreover, 89 percent of these ships have been constructed within the last two decades.

The Russians have deliberately avoided the giant supertanker and container freighter. Rather have they concentrated on the medium size cargo ship and the small tanker. They have the largest passenger fleet, some 70 liners, in the world.

Such a fleet certainly does serve commercial purposes. Sixty percent of Soviet imports are carried in Russian ships. The Russians have entered actively into the international carrying trade, much valuable hard currency is earned thereby as well as from the passenger service. The smaller Russian ships are well suited for trading in the ports of underdeveloped countries.

But such merchant ships can also be converted to serve military needs swiftly and efficiently. Indeed, at least 370 cargo ships and 112 tankers are designed and equipped to function immediately in the long range military role.[37] For military purposes the 45 Roll-On/Roll-Off freighters are particularly useful. These ships can carry vehicles and equipment in their holds secure from prying eyes and disgorge their cargo by a stern ramp without benefit of port facilities. Barge carriers, with cargo in barges unloaded by a stern elevator and small tugs, can disgorge 25,000 tons in 13 hours.

Soviet merchant ships carried military cargoes to North Vietnam during the war in Southeast Asia. Weapons and equipment have also been shipped to the Arab states in the Middle East. Arms and supplies, as well as Cuban and other troops, were transported to Angola and Ethiopia by Russian merchant shipping. Most important of all, as William H. Cracknell emphasizes:

> The Merchant Marine, on a regular basis, provides a significant amount of the logistics support required by the Soviet Navy, particularly to those ships operating in waters distant from the U.S.S.R. . . . Additionally, these merchant ships have a much greater freedom of access to the ports of the world than do navy ships or auxiliaries and thus can purchase fresh water, produce and other supplies for naval use in ports where warship visits might be denied.[38]

In the past, Soviet naval power has been sharply constricted by four major factors: lack of a carrier air force, an inability to refuel and resupply warships underway, inadequate open ocean antisubmarine capability, and lack of ready access to the open seas.

The Tu-26 is a quantum leap in the capabilities of Russian land based airpower and is viewed as a serious threat to U.S. super carriers. Wherever possible land based tactical air units could be coordinated to support Soviet naval efforts. But the lack of conventional carrier airpower remains a severe limitation on Soviet fleet operations.

Substantial progress in refueling while underway at sea has been registered by the Soviet Navy.[39] But the transfer of solids, such as ammunition, food, and spare parts, is largely done while at anchorages. However new Soviet warships are far better designed to refuel

alongside and receive sold provisions. Ten modern
fleet replenishment ships of the Chilikin and Dubna
classes have been brought into service in the 1970s.
The demands of possible sustained conflict are
compelling the USSR to make progress, however slowly,
in the exacting techniques of underway replenishment.

The ability of the Soviet fleet to find U.S.
submarines deployed in the open ocean remains limited.
But the quantum improvement in performance and armament
represented by the Alfa class will make it much more
difficult for US submarines. In situations where U.S.
carrier battle groups are committed to specific areas,
the task of US submarine escorts can be considerably
complicated by the sheer numbers of new Russian
submarines.

The division of the Soviet Navy into fleets
separated by vast distances does remain a handicap.
But the Russians have shifted their high seas fleets to
bases in the Arctic and the Soviet Far East. The
Baltic Fleet is configured and equipped to support army
operations along the coast. The primary purpose of the
Black Sea Fleet is to sustain operations in the
Mediterranean and a significant number of warships are
usually on duty in the eastern Mediterranean.

It is to the Northern and Pacific Fleets that one
must look to find the concentrations of major warships.
A vast complex of naval bases and installations has
been built on the Kola Peninsula around Murmansk.
Here, in July 1982, were stationed 75 major warships,
140 attack submarines, and 80 bombers.[40]

But the most dramatic expansion currently underway
is to be seen in the Pacific Fleet. An array of naval
complexes is to be found at Vladivostok and on the
Kamchatka Peninsula. Naval tonnage in the Pacific
increased 18 percent from 1977 to 1980.[41] By July 1982
the Pacific Fleet numbered 85 major warships, two Naval
Infantry regiments, 95 attack submarines, and 330
combat aircraft.[42] Comparing the two major Soviet
fleets, Bruce W. Watson concludes:

> The Pacific Fleet, however, had more major
> surface combatants, large amphibious ships,
> mine warfare ships and approximately 28
> percent of the total naval aircraft inventory.
> With 121,000 men, the Pacific Fleet was the
> largest of the four fleets in terms of
> manpower.[43]

A second major way in which the USSR has sought to
surmount geographical disadvantages is through securing
bases on the open oceans. Russian ships do use such
key ports as Luanda and Lobito Bay in Angola and Maputo
in Mozambique. There are strong indications that the
Soviets are on the verge of starting construction of

naval facilities at Luanda and Maputo. Other African
ports also beckon. In southern Angola Baia dos Tigres
would make a superb submarine base covering the south
Atlantic.[44] In Mozambique Nacala would provide a
comparable submarine base commanding the channel
between Africa and Madagascar.

Undoubtedly the most valuable windfall for the
USSR, however, is the naval base of Cam Ranh Bay in
Vietnam. Ironically, of course, these installations
were built by the United States during the war in
Southeast Asia. Today Cam Ranh Bay is known as
"Vladivostok South." The Russians have improved the
facilities substantially. Basic maintenance can be
performed on all classes of Soviet warships. Nuclear
fueled submarines can be serviced.

Cam Ranh Bay is extremely useful to the USSR for
many reasons. It is a warm water base on open ocean.
It is two days steaming distance into the Indian Ocean,
not seven days as is the case with Vladivostok. Soviet
naval power can swiftly be brought to bear on the
nearby vital sealane "choke points" of the Malacca,
Lombok, and Sunda Straits.

Serious deficiencies continue to limit Soviet naval
capabilities. But the Russians are tenaciously working
to remedy their shortcomings. In the years ahead, the
Soviet Navy may well prove to be an innovative and
increasingly formidable force.

1. Labayle Couhat, pp. 581-583.

2. Ibid.

3. Captain William H. Cracknell, ed., Understanding Soviet Naval Devlopments (Washington, D.C.: Office of the Chief of Naval Operations, Department of the Navy, January 1981), p. 22.

4. Ibid., p. 23.

5. Michael MccGwire, "Soviet Naval Doctrine and Strategy," in Derek Leebaert, ed., Soviet Military Thinking (London: George Allen & Unwin, 1981), p. 172.

6. Watson, p. 183.

7. Charles C. Petersen, "Trends in Soviet Naval Operations," in Bradford Dismukes and James M. McConnell, eds., Soviet Naval Diplomacy (New York, New York: Pergamon Press, 1979), p. 76.

8. Captain J.W. Kehoe and K.S. Brower, "US and Soviet Weapon System Design Practices," International Defense Review, June 1982, pp. 708, 711.

9. Labayle Couhat, pp. 593-596.

10. Cracknell, p. 33.

11. Labayle Couhat, pp. 616-619.

12. Ibid.

13. Captain J.W. Kehoe and K.S. Brower, "The Kirov," International Defense Review, February 1981, p. 156.

14. Labayle Couhat, p. 619.

15. Ibid., p. 630.

16. Ibid., pp. 628-630.

17. Rear Admiral Sayre A. Swarztrauber, "The Potential Battle of the Atlantic," in Frank Uhlig, ed., Naval Review 1979 (Annapolis, Maryland: U.S. Naval Institute, 1979), p. 114.

18. Labayle Couhat, p. 606.

19. Ibid., p. 584.

20. Ibid., p. 609.

54

21. Ibid., p. 608.

22. Ibid., p. 612.

23. Hansen, p. 84.

24. Labayle Couhat, p. 659.

25. The International Institute for Strategic Studies, The Military Balance 1982-1983, p. 16.

26. Ibid.

27. "Yakovlev 36MP," Air International, January 1979, pp. 18-20.

28. Ibid., p. 19.

29. Michael MccGwire, "Soviet Naval Doctrine and Strategy," p. 180.

30. The International Institute for Strategic Studies, The Military Balance 1982-1983.

31. "Backfire," Air International, June 1979, p. 308.

32. "Washington Roundup," Aviation Week & Space Technology, 23 August 1982, p. 13.

33. Gunston, pp. 377-378.

34. "Backfire Proliferates," Air International, October 1980, p. 188.

35. Clarence A. Robinson, Jr., "Backfire Threat Spurs F-14 Upgrading," Aviation Week & Space Technology, 30 August 1982, p. 49.

36. Cracknell, p. 61.

37. Hansen, p. 81.

38. Cracknell, pp. 62-63.

39. Ibid., p. 26.

40. The International Institute for Strategic Studies, The Military Balance 1982-1983.

41. "The Soviets Stir Up the Pacific," Time, 23 March 1981, p. 54.

42. The International Institute for Strategic

Studies, <u>The Military Balance 1982-1983</u>.

43. Watson, p. 143.

44. L.H. Gann and Peter Duignan, <u>Africa South of the Sahara: The Challenge to Western Security</u> (Stanford, California: Hoover Institution Press, 1981), p. 84.

VI
U.S. Mobile Forces and the Defense of Western Interests

How can the United States and its allies defend their vital interests in the Indian Ocean and Africa?

In the era following the Second World War western interests in these areas were secured by the armed forces of Great Britain and France. But a trip hammer succession of economic disasters overwhelmed Britain in the mid-1960s and the English were compelled to review their fundamental military and foreign commitments. Consequently, the British were largely forced to abandon their military presence "East of Suez". Fortunately Great Britain did retain the island base of Diego Garcia in the Indian Ocean, without which the current U.S. stratgic position in that area would be impossible.

France, in spite of painful ordeals, has maintained a military position in the Indian Ocean. Indeed, before the superpowers entered this arena, the French fleet was the largest exogenous naval force in the Indian Ocean. Even today the largest western ground force in the area is the Foreign Legion contingent in Djibouti.

But clearly the entry of the USSR and its partners into the African and Indian Ocean areas created a situation with which the French could not cope alone. In the wake of the war in Southeast Asia the U.S. armed forces were too preoccupied with internal problems to assume burdens in the Indian Ocean. Hence U.S. policymakers attempted to build Iran into a regional military power with a substantial infusion of U.S. weaponry and training. Such an effort appeared to be successful in the early and mid-1970s. But opposition within Iran to the Shah's oppressive and too "western" regime mounted rapidly in the late 1970s. A succession of disastrous blows shattered the edifice of United States policy in the Indian Ocean area. The Iranian Revolution, the seizure of the United States' Embassy in Teheran, and the Soviet invasion of Afghanistan forced the United States to bring U.S. armed forces

57

into the Indian Ocean in strength.

Deploying U.S. forces into the Indian Ocean is a staggering task. Such forces must travel 7000 nautical miles by air or 12,000 nautical miles by sea from the continental United States. To supply forces so committed is a logistical nightmare if there ever was one.

The concept of a mobile force, based in the United States and deployed overseas by air and sealift, however, is not new. Such a force was considered during the Kennedy administration.[1] The motives for assembling a rapidly deployable force were quite different in that era. It was then thought that much money, spent on stationing troops permanently overseas, could be saved. It was also hoped that a versatile force, capable of dealing with a wide range of contingencies, could be created. All of these plans were, however, engulfed in the Southeast Asian conflict where a major U.S. expeditionary force was committed.

In the 1970s U.S. forces were compelled to focus their efforts in western Europe and Korea. But a study in 1977 sought to develop a means of coping with "brushfire" conflicts that might erupt outside of NATO and Korea. In that year, President Carter issued Presidential Directive 18 ordering the formation of a mobile force comprising two Army divisions and one Marine division. But planning and developing such a force was a very desultory process. Indeed, so low did such a mobile force rank in military priorities that when the U.S. Army searched for maps of Iran, following the toppling of the Shah, there were none to be found and suitable topographical charts had to be borrowed from the British.[2]

Events in 1979 and 1980 swiftly transformed the situation. In an atmosphere of emergency a multiservice Rapid Deployment Joint Task Force was established in March 1980 with its Headquarters at MacDill Air Force Base near Tampa, Florida. At first the Force was, rather awkwardly, placed under the U.S. Army Readiness Command. In October 1981, however, the Force gained an independent status and reported directly to the Joint Chiefs of Staff in the chain of command.

Initially the effectiveness of the RJDTF has suffered from sharp infighting between the services.[3] Normal interservice rivalry has been exacerbated by fierce competition for important roles and budget funds. But the command problem fraught with most potential hazard was the assignment of the Indian Ocean to the U.S. Pacific Command headquartered in Hawaii while the Persian Gulf area was allocated to the U.S. European Command. But these problems are being resolved. Sensibly, the Army and the Marine Corps will rotate top command of the Force between them.

Logically, a U.S. Central Command has been officially created in January 1983. The new Command will place the region on a basis of equality with the European and Pacific Commands.

From its inception the RJDTF has been tasked with responsibility for operations in the Persian Gulf and Southwest Asian areas. With the dramatic Soviet occupation of Afghanistan in view, the top priority of the Force has been to deter further Soviet moves in these regions. Soviet aggression however, is not the only concern. Indeed a number of events have apparently convinced policymakers that outright Russian attack may be the least likely contingency and that the threats most likely to materialize are those of internal subversion.[4] These events included the assassination of President Anwar Sadat of Egypt and the narrow escape of the government of Bahrain from overthrow at the hands of Moslem extremists. The Libyan incursion into Chad and the activities of Ethiopian armed and trained guerrillas in Sudan seemed to target the Sudanese government from within and without. To these concerns was added, in the summer of 1982, the worry that Iran might seek to punish the Arab nations of the Gulf for their support of Iraq in the Iran-Iraq War. So the RDJTF, in the course of events, assumed responsibility for coping with a wide array of subtle and diverse threats and contingencies. Above all, it should be emphasized, the role of rapid deployment forces is to deter threats, both external and internal, within these vital regions. United States forces will be committed into an indigenous country only when invited.[5]

In order to deter, however, a force must present convincing evidence of an ability to fight effectively. No new formations have been created for the Central Command, rather forces in being are drawn upon. Such forces would be appropriately tailored to meet the particular demands of a given situation and threat. Flexibility and versatility are the keynotes of the Force. A number of the units listed for the Central Command, however, have a prior commitment to reinforce NATO or Korea. In the event of a far flung crisis those formations may not be available for service in Southwest Asia.

But a number of key units are now specifically earmarked for the Command, and in the event of need would come under operational control of the theatre commander. These units comprise: the 82d Airborne Division, the 101st Air Assault Division, and five Tactical Fighter Wings of the U.S. Air Force.[6] In addition, a Marine Amphibious Force, including an air wing, and the 7th Marine Amphibious Brigade are earmarked for service with the Command. Naval forces available for Indian Ocean duty include three carrier

battle groups, one amphibious group, and five squadrons
of long range ASW patrol aircraft. It must be noted,
however, that one of the carriers deployed in the
Indian Ocean was drawn from the Mediterranean fleet and
a second was forwarded from the Pacific. The United
States cannot always weaken commitments in other areas
in order to buttress its position in the Indian Ocean.
Given enough time and sealift, the 24th Mechanized
Infantry Division can be brought into operation.

Thirteen maritime prepositioning ships have been
stationed at Diego Garcia. These ships are crammed
with equipment and weapons for the 7th Marine Brigade
including 36 cannon, 53 M-60 battle tanks, 95
amphibious vehicles, and 582 trucks.[7] In addition
enough fuel, ammunition, and water are stockpiled on
the ships to sustain the 11,200 man Marine unit plus
some Air Force formations in combat for more than four
weeks.[8]

What U.S. forces can be most swiftly committed to
the Persian Gulf and Indian Ocean? What if the
government of Saudi Arabia should call for U.S. aid?

Within hours F-4 and F-15 fighter and F-111 strike
squadrons would be operating from well defended
airbases in Turkey and, as quickly as possible, Saudi
Arabia itself. An 1,800 man Marine Amphibious Unit is
an integral opart of the U.S. fleet in the Indian
Ocean. It would land along the Persian Gulf and move
northwest on Riyadh. The U.S. fleet in the
Mediterranean would dispatch its 1,200 man MAU by
helicopter to secure the airbase at Medina and advance
east on Riyadh. These Marine forces would be landed
and into action within 36 hours. Meanwhile a battalion
of 82d Division paratroopers would be dropped within 48
hours, to secure the most crucial airbases. A full
brigade of the 82d could be on the scene by the end of
four days.

Two other airborne formations may also be
available. Barring conflict between Egypt and Israel,
the battalion of the 82d with the multi-national
peacekeeping force in the Sinai could be rapidly
deployed elsewhere in the Middle East. Stationed in
northern Italy is a reinforced paratroop battalion with
its own dedicated airlift. This Airborne Task Force is
especially trained in mountain warfare and is augmented
by engineers skilled in demolition. It is also capable
of extremely rapid response. If its services are not
needed in NATO's southern theatre, the ATF could
quickly block vital mountain passes and roads in, for
example, Iraq or Iran.

What other troops can be brought in to reinforce
the units initially committed? The 11,200 men of the
7th Marine Brigade will be flown from California to
Diego Garcia, collect their equipment, and then enter
the fray. The 6th Air Cavalry Attack Brigade could be

swiftly brought on the scene. Configured as a helicopter tank killer unit, the 6th ACAB would be an especially welcome counter to Soviet bloc armor. Combat elements of the 101st Air Assault Division could be committed in two weeks. The 24th Mechanized Infantry, 17,900 men, could be brought to bear. But the tanks, armored personnel carriers, and self-propelled howitzers of the 24th must come by sea, a long journey requiring 30 to 35 days.

Although the forces earmarked for the Central Command are not massive in numbers, it must be noted that professionalism, discipline, and training count very heavily in combined operations over vast distances. The triumph of elite British forces against numerical odds in the Falkland Islands War is convincing proof of the value of professional troops. Moreover there is a limit to the forces that can be supplied and sustained -- even provided with enough fresh water -- in such immense and forbidding areas as Africa and the Middle East.

The United States does not lack troops. U.S. forces do need new organization to be effective in a rapid deployment role. At present many U.S. formations are designed to fight in the European theatre and are equipped with heavy vehicles pre-positioned in NATO countries. Certain types of more effective equipment and weapons are needed as well, such as a light armored vehicle with an anti-tank gun.

But the greatest disadvantage handicapping the United States is the sheer distance from North America to the Indian Ocean. Lack of enough airlift and sealift is the most critical constraint on U.S. operations. More U.S. troops could be more quickly deployed and sustained in action if enough transport planes and ships were in service.

Bases are especially crucial in the deployment of forces to far distant theatres. The impact of troops, particularly foreign soldiery, upon civilian populations always poses problems. Such problems are even more difficult and delicate when the societies are small in number and traditional in values, as is the case with many of the nations in Arabia and the Gulf.

Fortunately, an uninhabited chain of coral islands in the possession of Great Britain has been made available to the United States as the main base in the Indian Ocean. Diego Garcia has been built into a major military base with a 12,000 foot runway, 13 prepositioned equipment and supply ships, a communications complex, integrated into the global U.S. Defense Communications Network, and an array of logistical installations.[9] Indispensable as Diego Garcia is, however, there is a limit to how much can be crammed onto 30 square miles. But the most serious disadvantage of Diego Garcia is its remote location, more than 2,000 miles from the Persian Gulf.

A far better strategic location is to be found in the Sultanate of Oman, in the Arabian peninsula, fronting on the Arabian Sea and the Straits of Hormuz, the gateway to the Persian Gulf. A quiet and unobtrusive British and U.S. presence is to be found in Oman. Pains are being taken to avert any affront to fundamentalist Moslem sensibilities or the Sultan's independent political stance. Consequently, U.S. forces are permitted to use bases in Oman but stationing of troops is forbidden.

Preserving a careful anonymity, 650 British officers are on duty with the Omani armed forces.[10] Royal Air Force pilots fly the Jaguar fighter bombers of the Sultan. Former British bases provide the main facilities for U.S. use. The most valuable of these is a former RAF base, Ras Abu Rasas, located on Masirah island close offshore. Ras Abu Rasas possesses an 8,200 foot runway and basic facilities for as many as 40,000 men.[11]

U.S. Navy Orion long range patrol aircraft fly routine missions between Diego Garcia and Seeb airport in Oman.[12] Fighters from U.S. carriers operate in and out of the Omani airbase at Thamarit.[13] A modern air defense radar system and a sophisticated electronic communications system are being installed in Oman by U.S. firms.[14]

With a relatively small fundamentalist Moslem population and a proud sense of independence, Saudi Arabia is another nation in a vital strategic location. Indeed Saudi Arabia is the most significant component in western strategic interests in the region. It has been the major source, of course, of oil imported by Japan, Western Europe, and the United States.

Unfortunately, Saudi oil fields and key installations are concentrated close to or on the coastline of the Gulf, and are thus quite vulnerable to air and sea attack. Consequently the Saudis have devoted a considerable amount of their oil profits and concentrated much of their manpower in substantial armed forces. They have also been the driving force in the Gulf Security Council, a coalition of the varied Arab nations bordering the Gulf.

Wisely, Saudi Arabia has initially concentrated on building the essential infrastructure to support a military system and on systematic training of its forces along U.S., British, and French lines.[15] In order to construct the bases and carry on the training, the Saudis have relied upon more than 4,000 U.S. technicians and officers, 2,000 English personnel, and quite a number of French technicians.[16]

Hence the Saudi armed forces are now in a position to absorb sophisticated modern weaponry and employ it effectively. Sixty two F-15 fighters, six K-3 tankers, and five Boeing E-3A AWACS aircraft will be delivered by the United States to the Saudi air force. The six Saudi airbases are also protected by U.S. built Hawk anti-aircraft missile batteries.

Nonetheless, U.S. planners are haunted by the example of Iran. Will Saudi Arabia become another Iran? The seizure of the Grand Mosque, albeit a fleeting episode, illuminated the internal vulnerability of the Saudi regime.

Yet, without control of the air, it would be impossible for U.S. ground forces to operate in the open terrain of the Gulf area. The importance of Saudi forces and facilities is highlighted by Anthony H. Cordesman:

> By 1985, the U.S. Air Force would be able to operate with well trained and equipped Saudi and other conservative Gulf air forces from a series of sheltered bases covering the entire Gulf, to use Saudi KC-3 tankers to refuel, to draw on Saudi missile stocks and support capabilities in the critical initial period before US airlift could bring in USAF support equipment and munitions, and to use an "in place" AWACS.[17]

Essential stepping stones to the Arabian peninsula, the Egyptian airfields at Cairo West and at Ras Banas on the Red Sea have been made available to U.S. forces. Again, no permanent stationing of U.S. troops will be countenanced. But the airbases can be utilized in time of crisis. Egypt has cooperated closely with the RDJTF in two major maneuvers held on Egyptian soil.

Twelve substantial exercises have been staged by the RDJTF since its inception. The most notable overseas maneuvers have been Bright Star '81 and its sequel, Bright Star '82. Such exercises are not only necessary to develop the capabilities of a force, they can be employed to deter actions inimical to western interests. Bright Star '82 is a case in point. The assassination of Egyptian President Anwar Sadat sent shock waves through North Africa. Libya intervened in Chad and occupied that country. In the southern Sudan, guerrillas, trained and supported from bases within Ethiopia, increased the tempo of their operations. During November and December of 1981, 4,500 U.S. troops maneuvered in Egypt, 500 U.S. soldiers operated in the Sudan, and 1,000 Marines landed on the shores of Oman. The pressures upon the Sudan abated.

United States rapidly deployable forces are designed to meet a threat when called upon. But a demonstrated ability to cope with a variety of threats may indeed deter the need to meet them.

1.   William W. Kaufman, <u>Planning Conventional Forces, 1950-1980</u>, (Washington, D.C.: The Brookings Institution, 1982), pp. 8-11.

2.   Michael R. Gordon, "The Rapid Deployment Force-Too Large, Too Small or Just Right for Its Task?" <u>National Journal</u>, 13 March 1982, p. 451.

3. Frank Greve, "Marine, Army rivalries rob U.S. Rapid Deployment Force of effectiveness," <u>Philadelphia Inquirer</u>, 6 February 1982, pp. 3-F-4-F.

4. George C. Wilson, "U.S. Shifts Mideast Military Policy," <u>Washington Post</u>, 15 February 1982, pp. 1-2.

5. Jay La Monica, "RDF's 'Bright Star'," <u>The Washington Quarterly</u>, Spring 1982, p. 113.

6.   Ibid.

7.   Record, p. 49.

8. Public Affairs Office, <u>Fact Sheet</u> (MacDill AFB, Florida, June 1982), pp. 7-8.

9. Squadron Leader J. Clementson, "Diego Garcia," <u>Journal of the Royal United Services Institute for Defense Studies</u>, June 1981, p. 36.

10. "U.S. quietly building bases for Navy task force, " <u>Norfolk Virginian-Pilot</u>, 7 March 1982, p. C-2.

11. Clementson, p. 34.

12. "U.S. quietly building bases for Navy task force."

13. Ibid.

14. Ibid.

15. Anthony H. Cordesman, "The Changing Military Balance in the Gulf and Middle East," <u>Armed Forces Journal International</u>, September 1981, p. 56.

16. Ibid.

17. Ibid., p. 60.

VII
Land Based
Tactical Airpower

In the open terrain, desert and high plateau, of the Middle East and much of Africa control of the air is an absolute prerequisite to effective operations on the ground. Both land and carrier based forces are needed to secure supremacy in the air. Different situations call for appropriate kinds of airpower. It is highly risky to dispatch super carriers into constricted waters, such as the Persian Gulf. In such areas land based air contingents are far more suitable. On the other hand, the British could never have attempted to regain the Falkland Islands without the employment of two light carriers. Had the English also kept in service their medium carrier with Phantoms, Buccaneers, and AEW Gannets, the Argentines might well have been deterred from the Falklands misadventure.

Strengths and vulnerabilities are unique to each type of airpower. It is the proud boast of the air force that an airfield on land cannot be sunk. However, no U.S. forces have ever been evicted from a U.S. carrier, and that painful fate has befallen U.S. air force bases in Morocco, Libya, and elsewhere. Even more fraught with evil consequences is dependence upon dictatorships, such as Turkey and the Philippines. United States carriers are indisputable "U.S. territory" wherever they may be deployed.

What is clearly needed is well thought out and thorough integration of all tactical airpower components into mutually supporting deployments and operations. Much planning to secure this end is now underway. Air Force E-3A AWACS aircraft and F-15 fighters will be based in South Korea, the Indian Ocean, and Iceland to work in close cooperation with Navy carrier based air.[1] Marine Corps fighter squadrons are also being funded for land basing in support of carrier operations in certain vital sealane areas.[2]

Given concrete runways to receive them, Tactical Air Command squadrons of the U.S. Air Force are the

most immediately responsive and rapidly deployable of
American forces. All U.S. warplanes can be refueled in
air by tankers, thus vastly improving the range and
speed with which they can be deployed. Fighter
squadrons are regularly dispatched to the European and
Far Eastern theatres to become familiar with potential
wartime arenas. Flying from Idaho, F-111s took only 19
hours to arrive in Korea during a crisis in 1976.[3] Air
National Guard and Air Force Reserve units are well
trained, practiced in distant deployment, and will
quickly give a good account of themselves when needed.
Bare base kits, containing power generators, portable
shelters, fuel storage containers, and mobile
electronic equipment, make it possible for squadrons to
operate under primitive conditions.

U.S. Air Force doctrine emphasizes centralized
command, decentralized implementation, and flexibility
in the employment of air power.[4] U.S. air doctrine also
stresses initiative and concentration of warplanes
against critical objectives. Hence, the USAF insists
upon airpower within a theatre coming under a single
air force commander.

Among the major air combat missions of air
superiority and counterair operations, air
interdiction, and close air support, air superiority
logically enjoys top priority with the Air Force.[5]
Mission priorities do depend, however, upon the demands
of tactical situations.

However, the historical circumstances of the era
from 1945 to 1970 focused USAF efforts upon deep
interdiction missions. The results of such
interdiction campaigns are hotly debated. The
fundamental character of the war in Southeast Asia did
not lend itself to an interdiction campaign. In action
against a highly mechanized foe, dependent upon
elaborate rear area infrastructure, and operating in
open terrain, the U.S. Air Force might well inflict
decisive blows.

In its combat aircraft the U.S. Air Force has
demanded advanced technology, electronic and avionic
sophistication, and high performance. Virtually all
Air Force warplanes are capable of performing their
missions in spite of bad weather, and some can operate
at night. Consequently the U.S. Air Force, in
appropriate circumstances, is a very effective but very
expensive asset.

For many years the Air Force emphasized
multi-mission warplanes. Such aircraft could be
employed to accomplish a variety of roles, as tactical
situations demanded. Flexibility, keynoted in air
force doctrine, can thus be achieved. The F-4E Phantom
is the prime example of a machine adapted to meet the
demands of many missions.

In the 1970s, however, a variety of factors

compelled the Air Force to call for a new generation of more specialized warplanes. Particularly influential factors were the new dimensions of Soviet airpower, the consequent necessity for an effective air superiority counter, and the need for an antidote to burgeoning Russian battle tank deployment. Hence the F-15 and F-16 air superiority fighters, the A-7 attack plane, and the A-10 tank killer emerged.

The array of tactical aircraft in U.S. service in July 1982 numbered 3,650.[6] This figure included aircraft of the Air National Guard and Air Force Reserve as well as those of the Tactical Air Command. U.S. tactical airpower suffers a numerical inferiority in comparison with its rapidly growing counterpart, Soviet Frontal Aviation. "Small size, however," John M. Collins avers, "creates an Achilles Heel for America, because only a fairly small proportion of our active forces remain unfettered, and reserves can respond in most cases only after congressional approval."[7]

Unfortunately numbers are important. Even the finest warplane cannot be in two places at the same time. Inasmuch as numbers are related to cost and cost in turn to complexity, a hot debate has erupted over the issue of simplicity vs. sophistication. Would it not be better to secure a larger number of simple and less costly fighters for the money now invested in a smaller number of highly sophisticated machines?

The issue is not easily resolved. There are some attractive light fighters, such as the Northrop F-20, entering the market. But even such a fighter as the F-16, originally designed as a relatively low cost clear weather warplane, has become much more complex -- and much more expensive. Indeed, a truly low cost modern aircraft is increasingly difficult to find. Why is this the case?

Soviet fighters and attack planes are no longer the simple antagonists they were twelve or fifteen years ago. New Russian warplanes can only be mastered by first class equipment. Even where a Soviet challenge need not be met, virtually every nation on earth has purchased modern weapons. For instance, the British were forced to confront Exocet missiles and Super Etendard attack planes in Argentine hands.

If weather everywhere in the world were sunny and bright, a clear weather fighter would be a winning proposition. In many areas where vital U.S. interests are at stake, especially in Western Europe and Northeast Asia, weather is abominable. During the long winter in Germany ceilings below 1,500 feet and visibility less than three miles prevail 80 percent of the time.[8] Sophisticated vision devices now allow ground armies to operate effectively at night.

Therefore warplanes must be equipped to fly and fight at night as well.

Moreover, U.S. warplanes must be capable of functioning from "bare-bones" bases in far flung corners of the globe. Such operations place a premium upon sophisticated avionic and electronic systems as integrated components of the warplane. Only so equipped can U.S. combat aircraft operate autonomously in remote and primitive conditions.

A very thorough and detailed study of alternative fighter types was undertaken in 1981. The study compared a clear weather machine, a fairly sophisticated warplane, and an all weather day and night fighter.[9]. The reasonably sophisticated machine cost 10 percent more than the simple fighter but could fly twice the missions. The all weather fighter cost 30 percent more than the clear weather plane but flew and fought four times as many missions.

Complex warplanes are thus a necessity. Design and engineering can, however, sharply reduce the cost of maintenance and dramatically increase the reliability of sophisticated aircraft. Strikingly successful results have been obtained in maintenance and reliability in a number of the new generation of combat planes. Thus are the costs of complex aircraft reduced over the long run.

Most of all, to secure needed numbers of fighters and reduce costs, quantity production and multi-year contracts are needed. The cost of any item is a function of numbers produced as well as complexity. Low production rates sustain or even raise the expense of manufacture as well as deny needed weapons to the armed forces. For example, in Fiscal Year 1981 the price of an F-15 fighter at an annual production rate of 30 would have been $22.2 million; on the basis of a 42 plane purchase, $20.1 million, and if bought at a rate of 60 fighters per year, the individual F-15 would have cost $13.32 million.[10]

For many years the mainstay of the Tactical Air Command has been the McDonnell Douglas F-4E Phantom, a heavy twin engine fighter bomber with a crew of two. Although the Phantom is being swiftly supplanted in TAC, it remains the backbone of the Air National Guard squadrons. It is still in wide use with the air arms of Great Britain, West Germany, Israel, Egypt, Iran, Spain, Greece, Turkey, Japan, and South Korea.

The Phantom features long range, substantial payload, avionic sophistication, and high speed; being capable of Mach 2.17 at 36,000 feet.[11] Armed with four radar homing Sparrow air to air missiles and equipped with a camera, magnifying optics and a small TV screen for identifying foes beyond visual range, the F-4E remains a respectable interceptor. The Phantom continues to be effectively employed in fighter bomber strike missions. In a hi-lo-hi mission profile, the F-4E can unleash 4,920 lbs. of bombs against a target 439 nautical miles distant.[12]

Another key representative of the older generation of combat aircraft is the General Dynamics F-111, a twin engine, two seat, variable geometry long range strike fighter. A very highly sophisticated machine, the F-111 can automatically fly at an altitude of 200 feet at supersonic speed through wretched weather, at night, and over rugged -- even mountainous terrain.[13] F-111s now also fly close air support missions when weather is so execrable that all other aircraft are grounded. The Russian Sukhoi Su-24 and the Anglo-West German-Italian Panavia Tornado emulate the all weather, low level capabilities of the F-111 but neither can match the range and payload of the U.S. machine.

In the vast distances of Africa and the Middle East, the F-111 can play an especially valuable role. The massive Soviet electronic installations in these regions are particularly vulnerable to F-111 very low level, high speed penetration attack. Logically, two of the five wings of tactical fighters assigned to the Central Command are F-111 units.

Backbone of the new generation of tactical fighters is the McDonnell Douglas F-15C Eagle, a twin engine, all weather, single seat warplane specifically designed for the air superiority role. The F-15 features low wing loading, much wing surface area for lift, very sophisticated electronics, and more power than weight.

In May 1981 the USAF had brought into service 589 Eagles out of a total order of 729, and was considering the acquisition of an additional 320 machines. Deployed overseas are Tactical Air Command F-15 wings in West Germany and Okinawa. F-15s are operational with the Israeli Air Force and are on order for Japan and Saudi Arabia.

Maneuverability, climb rate, and acceleration performance make the F-15 an air superiority fighter without peer in the world, a record proven in combat by the Israeli Air Force. The Eagle is armed with an integral 20mm. machine cannon, four AIM-7F radar homing air to air missiles, and four AIM-9L all aspect infra-red homing air to air missiles.[15] Pulse-doppler radar enables the pilot to detect targets far away or flying very low. An advanced head-up display and an array of switches on throttle and stick make it possible for the pilot to control radar and weapons without distracting attention from flying and fighting.

A new C version of the F-15 features a number of improvements. The structure of the warplane is even stronger than before.[16] Improved radar provides a detailed picture of an enemy formation.[17] A new programmable radar signal processor enables the radar to track one target while simultaneously searching for others and transfer lock-on from one foe to another immediately.[18] Internal fuel has been increased by 2,000 lbs. to 13.455 lbs. Especially designed conformal fuel tanks can carry fuel or a variety of sensors or electronic gear without denigrating performance. Fitted with two such Fast Packs holding 9,750 lbs. of fuel, the ferry range of the F-15C -- without refueling in air -- is an astonishing 3,000 miles.[19] Little wonder an F-15C wing is earmarked for rapid deployment service.

Initially the new engines, extremely powerful -- each 23,904 lbs. thrust with afterburning, were quite troublesome and went through a protracted "teething" period. These difficulties, however, have finally been surmounted. Engine stalls have fallen from 1.5 per 1,000 engine hours in early 1980 down to less than one per 1,000 engine hours by the end of 1981.[20] During 1981 the Eagle boasted the highest readiness rate of all U.S. Air Force fighters and enjoyed the lowest accident rate.[21]

A large and powerfully engined warplane, the F-15 offers an excellent basis for development in the reconnaissance and long range strike roles. Currently under development is the F-15E, a two seat version armed with a 30mm. cannon pod, Maverick or Harpoon air to surface missiles or 2,000 lb. guided bombs.

Employing the new synthetic aperture radar a building the size of a house can be seen almost 56 miles away and a tank can be viewed more than 33 miles distant -- even in dismal weather.[22] The information gleaned from radar can then be fed into the navigation system, the radar switched off, and a low level attack can be made against the foe, undetected by enemy radar or passive warning systems.

The full potential of the F-15 in its air superiority role will not be realized, however, until a suitable "fire and forget" medium range air to air missile is brought into service. U.S. pilots must illuminate an enemy plane with radar until the AIM-7F Sparrow is close enough to the target to home on it. A fully active radar homing air to air missile is being developed by the United States and will certainly be welcomed by U.S. fliers.

In sheer numbers, however, pride of place will belong to the General Dynamics F-16 Fighting Falcon. Tactical Air Command and Air National Guard squadrons will be equipped with 1,995 F-16s. In April of 1981 the USAF had taken delivery of 400 F-16As.[23] Moreover, the F-16A is the major warplane for Belgium, the Netherlands, Denmark and Norway, being assembled in Belgian and Dutch factories as well as United States. The F-16A has proven itself in combat with the Israeli Air Force, deliveries are underway to Egypt, and Pakistan, South Korea, and Venezuela have put in orders for the sleek fighter.

The F-16 is one of the few U.S. combat aircraft whose production could be steeply increased if need demanded. One of the largest military factories in the world, the Fort Worth plant turns out ten F-16s each month. But more than 20 Fighting Falcons per month could be easily manufactured, and, with additional tooling, the rate could reach 45 a month.[24]

In operations and maneuvers the F-16A has etched a remarkable record. A Fighting Falcon unit was dispatched to Norway to operate for almost a month in the northern winter.[25] The unit required only ten hours and two refuelings to fly from Utah to Norway. Once at the Norwegian airbase, only two hours and thirty six minutes were needed to prepare the F-16s for combat. Pilots flew from runways slick with ice, snow, and slush. Intensive operations were flown by the F-16s with minimum maintenance and no spare parts on hand.

In the annual Royal Air Force tactical bombing competition, an F-16A contingent won first place, defeating RAF Buccaneer and Jaguar and USAF F-111 units.[26] RAF Lightnings and Phantoms sought to intercept the F-16s. In vain, as F-16s "shot down" 86 of their opponents for no loss of their own. The Fighting Falcons earned 7,831 out a maximum 8,000 points for accurate bombing.

In Israeli service F-16As, each carrying two 2,000 lb. bombs and external fuel tanks, flew 600 miles to attack and demolish a nuclear reactor near Baghdad, Iraq. In the War in Lebanon F-16s shared equally with F-15s in the slaughter of Syrian flown MiG-21s and MiG-23s.[27]

Originally the F-16 was designed as a clear weather extremely maneuverable "dogfighter", a relatively low cost supplement to the F-15. But a clear weather fighter is virtually useless in Europe, and in much else of the world as well. The Belgians, Dutch, and Scandinavians needed a versatile fighter bomber as well as a "dogfighter".

Hence the F-16 has become a sophisticated machine capable of functioning in miserable weather and extremely accurate in ground attack. Many innovations in design and engineering make the Fighting Falcon an incredible agile and quick fighter, as RAF Lightning and Phantom and Syrian MiG "jockeys" can attest.

The F-16A is capable of 1,350 miles per hour at 40,000 feet and 915 miles per hour at sea level.[28] In the air superiority role, the Fighting Falcon is armed with an integral 20mm. machine cannon and four AIM-9L Sidewinder infra-red homing air to air missiles. Flying a typical hi-lo-hi profile attack mission, the F-16A carries six 500 lb. bombs and can attack a target 340 miles distant. Supplementary fuel tanks, of course, greatly augment operating radius.

Employing the sam engine as the F-15, the F-16 has been afflicted by the same protracted developmental difficulties that beset the Eagle. Otherwise the F-16 has proven to be a highly reliable, remarkably self-contained, and easily maintained plane. It is, technicians avow, one of the easiest aircraft on which to work, quick access doors make components easy to service and replace.

Progressive avionic and electronic improvements are being incorporated into successive "blocks" of planes as they come into production. Such improvements are manifold, but include such elements as a new radar, a new head-up display, increased use of graphite epoxy in the structure, and a five fold increase in the capabilities of the weapons control computer.[29]

Currently under test is a version, designated F-16XL, configured for the strike interdiction role. It features a cranked arrow wing, doubling the wing area and expanding fuel capacity, lift, and payload. The new wing design minimizes drag at high subsonic speeds yet does not exact a penalty in maneuverability. A General Electric 28,000 lb. thrust engine is being tested in an F-16XL as well. The goal is to develop an F-16E able to carry twice the payload of the A model a distance 40 percent greater.[30]

The F-16A lacks the long distance radar target tracking capability of the F-15. Nor does the Fighting Falcon possess the Eagle's "look down, shoot down," advantage. A deficiency that should be corrected, however, is the inability to fire AIM-7F radar homing air to air missiles. Lacking medium range missiles, the F-16A is forced to close on its foe in combat -- and is thus a target for enemy medium range rockets. The F-16C, comprising the last 603 Fighting Falcons, will be armed with the new "fire and forget" medium range air to air missile.[31] Meanwhile, however, F-16s should be fitted with Sparrows.

Unique in the history of U.S. Air Force annals is the Fairchild Republic A-10A Thunderbolt II, a twin engine, single seat highly specialized flying tank destroyer. When production is completed in April 1984, 707 A-10s will have been manufactured.[32] Twelve TAC and five ANG and Reserve squadrons operated A-10s in mid-1982.[32] Six of these squadrons are posted to England and West Germany.

The A-10A is dedicated to the destruction of enemy armor wherever it may be encountered in strength. Designed to fly and fight at 100 feet -- and less -- the Thunderbolt is built with survivability uppermost in mind. Mounted on top of the fuselage, the twin engines are shielded from anti-aircraft fire. Protective foam lines the fuel tanks. Flight control systems are redundant and widely separated. Extensive use is made of titanium armor to shield the pilot and vital elements of the aircraft. Shells from 23mm. and even 37mm. cannon cannot penetrate the Thunderbolt's titanium "hide".[37]

To kill tanks, the A-10 employs a seven barrel 30mm. machine cannon mounted internally. This weapon fires a heavy armor piercing incendiary round with devastating impact.[35] Twenty anti-armor cluster bombs are also part of the Thunderbolt's arsenal of anti-tank weapons.

In the close support mission the Thunderbolt has a range of 576 miles with a two hour loiter time. Deployment to distant arenas is readily possible with a ferry range of 2,647 miles.[36] The A-10 may well be the U.S. "ace in the hole" against enemy armor in Southwest Asia and Africa as well as Western Europe.

No account of modern airpower would be complete without emphasis upon AWACS, airborne warning and control systems. The modern air battlefield is a highly sophisticated electronic arena. At 40,000 feet, USAF Boeing E-3A Sentry airborne radar can pick up enemy planes 250 miles distant and can track 240 aircraft simultaneously. The Gumman E-2C Hawkeye performs the same role for the US Navy and the Israeli Air Force. Defending fighters are computer guided by these AWACS machines to intercept the foe. In the Lebanon War Israeli Hawkeyes detected Syrian fighters at the moment of take off and vectored the nearest F-15s and F-16s to engage and shoot down the MiGs.[37]

Land based tactical airpower is thus one of the strongest cards the United States has to play. Employed in appropriate circumstances it can indeed be a decisive instrument.

It is, however, necessarily an expensive tool. There are no cheap "short-cuts" in modern airpower. In a number of situations, moreover, airpower is simply not relevant. In some circumstances airpower can be counter-productive and wantonly destructive. Above all, land bases in many areas are at the mercy of unstable political conditions or repugnant dictatorships.

Tactical airpower must be selectively employed. This is no easy task, organizational pressure to play a part in any conflict is very strong. Warplane costs can be substantially reduced through volume production of key types. Above all, land based air forces must be thoroughly integrated into an overall framework which embraces all elements of tactical airpower.

1. Clarence A. Robinson, Jr., "DeLauer Urges Technology Spending," Aviation Week & Space Technology, 6 September 1982, p. 263.

2. Clarence A. Robinson, Jr., "Defense Decision Hikes Strategic Funds," Aviation Week & Space Technology, 23 August 1982, p. 19.

3. Collins, p. 223.

4. United States Air Force, Air Force Manual 1-1, Functions and Basic Doctrine of the United States Air Force (Washington, D. C.: Headquarters USAF/XOX, February 1979), pp. 5-2, 5-6.

5. Collins, p. 222.

6. The International Institute for Strategic Studies, The Military Balance 1982-1983, p. 8.

7. Collins, p. 237.

8. Benjamin F. Schemmer, "Exclusive AFJ Interview: Commander in Chief, USAFE, and Commander, AAFCE, General Charles A. Gabriel," Armed Forces Journal International, January 1982, p. 35.

9. Deborah G. Meyer, "The Simplicity vs. Complexity Issue," Armed Forces Journal International, January 1982, p. 46.

10. Benjamin F. Schemmer, "USAF Tac Air at Modernization/Readiness Threshold." Armed Forces Journal International, January 1981, p. 46.

11. "Five Grand Fighter," Air International, November 1978, p. 215.

12. Ibid., pp. 212-213.

13. Craig Covault, "F-111 Fighter Role Being Expanded," Aviation Week & Space Technology, 6 February 1978, p. 119.

14. Roy Braybrook, "New Roles For The F-15 Eagle," Air International, August 1981, pp. 61,83.

15. Ibid., p. 63.

16. David R. Griffiths, "F-15 Pilots Cite Need for New Air-to-Air Missile," Aviation Week & Space Technology, 2 November 1981, pp. 52-53.

17. Ibid.

18. Braybrook, p. 64.

19. "Conformal Fuel Tanks Increase Range of F-15," Aviation Week & Space Technology, 26 April 1982, p. 27.

20. Griffiths, p. 53.

21. "F-15s Used for Air Defense Intercepts," Aviation Week & Space Technology, 7 June 1982, p. 69.

22. Braybrook, pp. 67-68, 82-83.

23. Alwyn T. Lloyd, "More Fight For The Fighting Falcon," Air International, October 1981, p. 161.

24. Ibid.

25. Erwin J. Bulban, "F-16s Deployed to Norway For Environmental Tests," Aviation Week & Space Technology, 11 May 1981, pp. 69-71.

26. Lloyd.

27. Clarence A. Robinson, Jr., "Surveillance Integration Pivotal in Israeli Successes," Aviation Week & Space Technology, 5 July 1982, p. 17.

28. Lloyd. p. 166.

29. Ibid., p. 162.

30. "F-16XL Readied for Flight Testing," Aviation Week & Space Technology, 5 July 1982 p. 15.

31. Lloyd.

32. "Congress Votes to Terminate A-10 Production," Aviation Week & Space Technology, 23 August 1982, p. 16.

33. The International Institute for Strategic Studies, The Military Balance 1982-1983, pp. 8-9.

34. "The Fairchild Can-Opener: Shturmovik of the Eighties?" Air International, June 1979, p. 270.

35. Ibid., p. 272.

36. Ibid., p. 287.

37. Cordesman, "The Sixth Arab-Israeli Conflict: Military Lessons for American Defense Planning."

VIII
Light Forces of
the U.S. Army

At the heart of the U.S. rapid deployment force are the light formations of the U.S. Army. These units are highly mobile and elements from them can be deployed to far corners of the world swiftly. A United States presence can thus be on the scene wherever such a commitment is deemed essential.

The 82d Airborne Division is the only U.S. paratroop division. Sixteen thousand soldiers are in the 82d Division. Nine paratroop infantry battalions are backed by three battalions of artillery, one battalion of light tanks, an air defense battalion, a helicopter battalion, and other supporting units.[1]

Anti-aircraft weapons include 18 towed Vulcan 20mm. machine cannon units in the air defense battalion and the Stinger man portable missile at infantry unit level. The division is furnished with 417 anti-tank missile launchers, Dragon medium and TOW heavy rocket weapons. Artillery firepower has been immensely improved by the replacement of 105mm. howitzers with new M-198 155mm. howitzers. Range of the M-198 is 24,000 meters and the piece can sustain a rate of fire of four rounds per minute. Fifty four of the new howitzers are to be found in the artillery battalions.

Another significant new asset is the Combat Electronic Warfare and Intelligence battalion. On the modern electronic battlefield the ability to mislead the enemy, disrupt his communications, and glean information is of critical importance. A CEWI contingent is being attached to each U.S. Army division.

A major shortcoming is to be seen in the Sheridan armored reconnaissance vehicle serving in the light tank battalion. While Sheridan is fully tracked and can be dropped by air, its 152mm. combined gun and missile launcher is an unmitigated disaster -- even a hazard to the crew. Indeed the vehicle was withdrawn from service except with the 82d. The Sheridan will be superceded by the new light armored vehicle selected by

77

the Army and the Marine Corps.

The 82d keeps a Division Ready Brigade, some 4,000 troops, on alert to respond quickly to any emergency.[2] The first of the DRB's three battalions can move out in 18 hours. Within 24 hours all of the brigade can be on its way.

Another key rapid deployment formation is the 101st Air Assault Division. Numbering 17,295 men at full strength the 101st is unique in its employment of 452 helicopters for mass movement and attack by air.[3] The 101st possesses the same artillery and air defense weaponry as the 82d. But anti-tank capability is immensely strengthened by the 111 Bell AH-IS Cobras in the attack helicopter units of the 101st.[4]

Air assault capabilities are greatly strengthened by the transition to the new Sikorsky UH-60 Blackhawk transport helicopter. The Blackhawk can carry far more troops and payload than the old "Huey" and is much faster and quite maneuverable. Most important of all, Blackhawk can function at full load at high altitudes and high temperatures -- a crucial matter in Southwest Asia and Africa.

But two critical constraints singularly handicap operations by the 101st. Helicopters now in service, even the new Blackhawk, must be carried by air transport to distant theatres. This problem is compounded by the bulkiness of helicopters which makes them inefficient cargo in transport aircraft. Moreover the United States suffers from a shortage of airlift.

It is true that the helicopter affords many unique combat capabilities. But helicopters demand a great deal of maintenance. Attack helicopters in particular devour fuel and ammunition. Scarce transport planes must thus be devoted to supporting helicopters deployed in primitive arenas far from the continental United States.

These two constraints apply with equal force to a new anti-tank unit, the Air Cavalry Attack Brigade. The first such formation, the Sixth ACAB, is dedicated to the Central Command. Two attack helicopter battalions, with 42 attack machines and 24 scout helos, make up the cutting edge of the brigade. Two cavalry companies, with 38 cavalry fighting vehicles, hold essential terrain. In turn they are shielded by two air cavalry companies employing eight attack and twelve scout helicopters.

The ACAB is indeed a formidable specialized anti-tank force. It is a radical departure from the traditional reconnaissance role of the cavalry. But the air transport and logistical burdens imposed by the ACAB are equally formidable. Deployment of an ACAB to Southwest Asia may not be realistically feasible until airlift has been substantially expanded.

In the course of the 1970s the U.S. Army had to

confront the threat of mushrooming numbers of Soviet bloc tanks and other armored vehicles in central Europe and in Korea. The U.S. Army was forced to cope with this growing armored phalanx while handicapped by a shortage of funds and volunteer soldiers, and compelled to secure new weapons for a vast array of equipment long overdue for replacement. Logically, under these circumstances, the Army stressed armored and mechanized infantry formations, and helicopter units as a highly mobile reserve. Understandably, "foot-slogging" infantry divisions were very low on the priority list and suffered accordingly.

When the events in Southwest Asia compelled the United States to form the RDJTF, a painful weakness was immediately apparent. Light U.S. infantry could arrive on the scene quickly by air. But lacking armor, they faced the prospect of speedy annihilation by enemy tank forces in the region. However main battle tanks are heavy and attack helicopters too bulky to be air transported in mass. Hence armor must be shipped by sea, a voyage consuming more than a month from the continental United States to the Indian Ocean area.

Now, of course, some main battle tanks are stockpiled at Diego Garcia for Marine units. The United States relies very heavily upon tactical airpower for anti-armor support. If and when airlift is greatly enlarged, attack helicopter units can be extremely useful. None of these measures, however, can be a viable substitute for effective air portable armor as an integral component of the infantry division.

The U.S. Army is now in the process of developing a new high technology light division that can be deployed by air and yet be able to hold its own against enemy armor. Such a model is evolving in the High Technology Test Bed at Fort Lewis, Washington.[5] Three infantry divisions: the 9th at Fort Lewis, the 7th at Fort Ord, California, and the 25th in Hawaii, will eventually be restructured along the pattern worked out by the HTTB.

Separate from, but obviously closely related to the HTTB, is a complex process of testing and selection of appropriate light armored vehicles.[6] This process involves selection of advanced vehicles to be secured in the future. Meanwhile, vehicles to fill the gap will be purchased from types currently available on the market. The program involves both the U.S. Army and the U.S. Marine Corps in a joint effort to secure effective light armored vehicles needed by both forces. Interim vehicles will number 969, 680 for the Army and 289 for the Marines.[7] Vehicles to be secured in the far term may number 1,100, 700 in Army service and 400 for the Marine Corps.[8]

The new model high technology light division will have five motorized infantry battalions employing the

interim light armored vehicle as an APC.[9] Two more
infantry battalions will be mounted on the new 1 1/4
ton high mobility multipurpose wheeled vehicles.
Another two battalions will be assault gun units
utilizing a version of the interim vehicle armed with a
cannon. An Air Cavalry Attack Brigade will be an
integral part of the division. An anti-tank company
will also be featured equipped with 24 TOW launchers
mounted on HMMWVs.

Two battalions in the artillery brigade will be
armed with 48 M-198 155mm. howitzers. The third
battalion will be equipped with the new Vought multiple
launch rocket system. Each MLRS launching unit can
unleash twelve rockets against targets 30,000 meters
distant in less than a minute.

The air defense battalion has mounted Chaparral
units on trailers, handy for air portability. The
Roland system is apparently too heavy for convenient
air transport. Currently, a variety of cannon are
being tested in a quest for an effective lightweight
anti-aircraft gun.

Quite apart from the light armored vehicle program,
HTTB is testing a variety of compact vehicles. These
include the Porsche Weasel tracked personnel carrier,
the Austrian Pinzgauer truck, and a compact
Mercedes-Benz engineering truck fitted with bulldozer
blade, backhoe, and bucket loader.[10]

At present it would require some 1,230 sorties to
deploy an infantry division from the United States
overseas. Such a movement would also require the use
of the giant C-5A transports. The goal of HTTB is to
reduce the sorties needed to transport the new light
infantry division to 1000, employing C-141Bs
exclusively.

The helicopter, transport and attack, has become a
thoroughly integral part of the U.S. Army's combined
arms team and strategic concepts of the Airland
conflict and the extended battlefield. Effective
defense against mass enemy armor, in particular,
depends very heavily upon attack helicopters. In the
offensive, enemy defenses can be leapfrogged by
heliborne infantry.

A new general purpose tactical transport
helicopter, the Sikorsky UH-60 Blackhawk, is rapidly
entering U.S. Army service. The Army will secure 1,107
Blackhawks, which will partly replace the aging Bell
"Huey".[11]

The Blackhawk can carry 14 troops or a 105mm.
cannon and crew.[12] It has been designed to be an
exceptionally reliable and easily maintained machine.
Many features enhance survivability; electric and
hydraulic systems are duplicated, a radar system alerts
the crew to an attack, and an infra-red jammer and
chaff dispenser can frustrate anti-aircraft missiles.

Armor protection is provided for the pilots. Main rotor bades can take 23mm. cannon hits and continue to function. Blackhawk is thus much more than simply a replacement for the "Huey". The attention focused on attack helicopters should not obscure the quantum leap in capabilities made possible by Blackhawk.

The medium lift helicopter in U.S. Army service is the Boeing Vertol CH-47 Chinook. Four hundred thirty nine CH-47s were operational in the spring of 1982. [13] Four hundred thirty six Chinooks are being modified to D model standards, 91 new Ds will be purchased to make up a total fleet of 527 Ch-47Ds. Almost 14 tons of cargo or 44 soldiers can be carried over a range of 230 miles by the Chinook.[14]

Crucial to the fortunes of the U.S. Army on the battlefield are the attack helicopters. In the spring of 1982, 1,091 Bell AH-1 Cobras were in service.[15] Cobras currently in the inventory are undergoing comprehensive modification to the quite sophisticated S model. Improvements include: a Doppler navigator, a head-up display, a fire-control computer, a laser range finder and target tracker, an engine exhaust cooler, and an infra-red jammer.[16] Incorporated into the S model is a chin turret mounting a three barrel 20mm. machine cannon, a much needed weapon against the Soviet Hind helicopter.

In the tank hunting role, the Cobra is armed with eight wire guided TOW missiles with a range of 3,750 meters. A Cobra usually needs 25 seconds to bring a tank into its TOW sight and 15 seconds to guide the missile to its target.[17] Fourteen unguided 70mm. rockets are also carried, to be loosed against the radar aeriels of quad 23mm. self-propelled anti-aircraft units. In a tank hunter mission, Cobras fly extremely low -- below the treetops -- and use all available cover. Mission endurance is approximately 1.9 hours.

The Cobra, when supplied with sufficient fuel and munitions, can be a formidable weapon against tanks. Even a Soviet Lieutenant General concedes, in an article in Red Star, that attack helicopters can inflict losses on tanks at a ratio of 12 to one or as high as 19 to one.[18] And the A-10 and Cobra in joint operations form an even more devastating team against enemy armor.

But the Cobra has been developed to the limit of its potential. Moreover the Cobra does have shortcomings. It has very limited capability for night action or bad weather operations. Worst of all, the Cobra is essentially configured for a 2000 foot altitude, 70° Fahrenheit environment. In the Middle Eastern or African 4,000 foot altitude and 95° Fahrenheit situation, the Cobra would be very seriously handicapped.

A far more powerful attack helicopter is the new Hughes AH-64, 515 of which the Army hopes to secure.[19] Main battery of the new Apache is 16 Hellfire missiles, semi-active laser homing anti-tank rockets with a range of some 7,000 meters.[20] The laser sight enables the gunner to hold a spot on target while the pilot maneuvers to evade anti-aircraft fire.[21] The Apache is also armed with the lethal 30mm. chain gun machine cannon. Stinger anti-aircraft missiles may be mounted as well.

Sophisticated electronic and avionic systems permit the AH-64 to fly and fight at night and in the worst of weather. The twin 1,690 shaft horsepower engines confer the needed ability to function at high altitudes and hot temperatures. It has been thoroughly tested in the heat and dust of the Arizona and California deserts. The Apache has sufficient ferry range to deploy, with refueling stages, from the continental United States to distant arenas.

Such capabilities do not come inexpensively however. Estimated flyaway cost of the AH-64 is approximately 9.5 million dollars.[22]

But it should be no surprise that high performance, all weather, very sophisticated helicopters should cost almost as much as comparable fixed wing warplanes. To be sure, Cobras can perform well in the European theatre. But if the Army is expected to be fully effective in Southwest Asia then a substantially improved attack helicopter may indeed be necessary.

Yet helicopters are bulky items to be shipped in large numbers by transport aircraft to far distant arenas. In action helicopters consume vast quantities of ammunition and fuel -- again straining airlift and sealift which is in short supply. Thus ground troops must have an armored vehicle readily and swiftly deployable by air.

An interim vehicle was selected at the end of summer 1982. Emerging the winner was a Swiss Mowag design, manufactured under license by General Motors of Canada for the Canadian Army. Powered by a 300 horsepower diesel engine, the Cougar, as it is designated in Canadian service, eight wheeled car weighs 13.8 tons combat loaded.[23] It is thus readily air portable by transport aircraft and Chinook helicopter. It is capable of a road speed of 68 miles per hour, can swim at six miles per hour, and has a road range of 430 miles.[24] High hardness steel armor plate is proof against 7.62mm. bullets and artillery fragments. In Canadian service, the Cougar has proven to be a particularly reliable vehicle with a high rate of availability. It is notable as well for ease of maintenance.

The U.S. Army will form ten armored car battalions, each fielding 42 cars.[25] Two of these battalions will be incorporated into the 82d Division, the 101st Division, and each of the three light divisions. The LAV-25, as it is termed in U.S. service, will be armed with a 25mm. machine cannon and be manned by a commander, gunner, and driver.[26] To be sure, bringing light armored vehicles into service will entail radical changes in U.S. Army organization and tactics. Yet the move by the U.S. Army to the new light division is to be encouraged. Equipped with light armor, the light division can assure the versatility and flexibility needed for effective operations in Third World arenas.

It is upon the Army that the United States must rely for large scale combat and sustained operations. Finally, resources are being made available to equip the U.S. Army for such essential roles in the Indian Ocean area as well as Central Europe and Korea. The new light division is a necessary organizational and tactical step in the right direction.

1. Collins, p. 210.

2. Dr. E. Asa Bates, "The Rapid Deployment Force-Fact or Fiction," Journal of the Royal United Services Institute for Defense Studies, June 1981, pp. 24-25.

3. 101st Airborne Division (Air Assault) Headquarters, Air Assault Structure Handbook (Fort Campbell, Kentucky: Headquarters, 101st Airborne Division (Air Assault), July 1982), p. 5.

4. Ibid.

5. Ramon Lopez, "The US Army's Future Light Infantry Division - a key element of the RDF," International Defense Review, February 1982, p. 185.

6. "International Defense Digest," International Defense Review, August 1982, pp. 973-974.

7. Ibid., p. 973.

8. Ibid., p. 974.

9. "HTTB Overview to Dr. Cordier," Headquarters, HTTB, Fort Lewis, Washington, 7 July 1982.

10. Lopez, p. 187.

11. Charles Gilson, "Some operational aspects of the UH-60A Black Hawk," International Defense Review, July 1980, p. 1067.

12. Ibid., p. 1069.

13. Deborah G. Meyer, "What's in the Army's Arsenal of Aircraft?"

14. Tom Gervasi, Arsenal Of Democracy (New York, New York: Grove Press, Inc., 1978), p. 148.

15. Deborah G. Meyer, "What's in the Army's Arsenal of Aircraft?"

16. Mark Lambert, "The US Army's Cobra Companies," International Defense Review, September 1981, pp. 1179-1180.

17. Ibid., p. 1181.

18. Lt. Col. E.J. Everett-Heath, "The Mi-24 Hind in an Anti-Helicopter Role," International Defense Review, September 1981, p. 1148.

19. "Advanced Military Needs Shaping Rotorcraft Gains," <u>Aviation Week & Space Technology</u>, 14 March 1983, pp. 62-63.

20. Deborah G. Meyer, "Interview with Major General Carl H. McNair, Jr.," <u>Armed Forces Journal International</u>, May 1982, p. 54.

21. Ibid., p. 50.

22. "House Armed Services Committee's Views," <u>Armed Forces Journal International</u>, May 1982, p. 27.

23. Captain Edwin W. Besch, USMC, "Light armored vehicles - needs and candidates," <u>Marine Corps Gazette</u>, December 1980, p. 40.

24. Ibid.

25. Lopez, p. 190.

26. Ibid.

IX
The Marine Corps

The United States Marine Corps is a unique body of
troops. It emphasizes a proud tradition, based upon a
remarkable record of achievement in war and peace. It
is a combined arms team of land, air, and sea elements
working in the closest integration and mutual support.
The amphibious assault capability of the Marine Corps
affords immense strategic flexibility, as the
outflanking campaigns of the Pacific in the Second
World War and the Inchon landing in the Korean conflict
attest. It is an elite light infantry force. As its
rival services can ruefully bear witness, the Marine
Corps possesses a powerful political base in strong
Congressional support.

A number of analysts have urged that the Marine
Corps should assume the entire responsibility for rapid
deployment missions, in accord with the adoption by the
United States of a dominant maritime strategy. Such
voices include Jeffrey Record, William S. Lind, a prime
mover in the "reform group" in Washington military
circles, and key Senators William S. Cohen and John
Tower.[1]

Could the Marines take up the exclusive
responsibility for the rapid deployment mission? To be
sure, the Marine Corps occupies a position of central
importance among the forces assigned to cope with
contingencies erupting in far corners of the globe. The
Marines rank among the finest light infantry in the
world, particularly proficient in small unit actions.
Above all, Marine capabilities in amphibious operations
endow the United States with a unique and invaluable
strategic advantage, the ability to outflank an enemy
from the sea. Obviously such a strategic option is of
crucial relevance in the Indian Ocean and African
arenas. It is true that the United States plans to
intervene in these areas only when invited to do so.
But evicting a hostile force thrusting deep into a
friendly government's territory may demand precisely
the ability to carry out amphibious assault which is

87

the forte of the Marine Corps.

But, even though the Marine Corps is strategically highly flexible, it is tactically extremely specialized and limited. The Marine Corps is not designed, organized, equipped or trained for long sustained combat, positional warfare, or battle against a heavily mechanized foe. The Marines lack significant armor, artillery, and logistical support for sustained operations. The Marines are even deficient in ground mobility. They are overwhelmingly dependent upon their own air force and helicopters for firepower and mobility. In order to meet the full range of possible missions in the rapid deployment role, the Marine Corps would have to be completely restructured, re-equipped, and retrained.

Rather than attempt to make of the Marine Corps something that it is not, the Marines should be supported in the missions for which they are organized and trained, and for which the Marines are uniquely qualified. Fortunately, significant moves are underway designed to address the shortcomings in needed equipment of the Corps. High on the priority list are heavy lift helicopters, AV-8B V/STOL close support fighter bombers, and light armored vehicles.[2] Funding is now available to add more heavy anti-tank missile launchers, 40mm. grenade launchers, .50 caliber machine guns, and other weapons; increasing Marine firepower by 25 percent.[3] In long run developments, badly needed new amphibious ships and air cushion high speed landing craft are being procured.[4]

Unique among U.S. armed forces, the strength of the Marine Corps is mandated by act of Congress at no less than three divisions and three air wings.[5] Size of the Corps thus remains quite stable. In July 1982 the Corps numbered 192,000 Marines and some 440 aircraft and 622 helicopters.[6] Many nations have Marine contingents but none possess so large a counterpart. Indeed the USMC is larger than the entire army of Great Britain.

Marine combat organization is also unique. Combat forces are formed on the basis of the "building block" principle, ad hoc combinations being woven together to meet specific mission requirements. Such extraordinary flexibility works because Marines share a superb esprit de corps, methods of operation are the same throughout the Corps, and training is intensive and realistic.

The basic "building block," of course, is the infantry battalion, an exceptionally large formation in Marine Corps practice. The smallest contingent usually deployed with U.S. fleets is the Marine Amphibious Unit, a battalion buttressed by artillery, tank, helicopter, and service support detachments.

Marine Amphibious Brigades are designed to meet more substantial combat demands. A MAB comprises two to five infantry battalions, an artillery battalion, a variety of other units, and a service support group. A MAB varies in size from 7,000 to 16,000 troops.[7] A Marine aircraft group is also an integral component of a MAB.

The largest formation fielded by the Corps is the Marine Amphibious Force which includes an infantry division, a tank battalion, an air wing, and support units -- as many as 52,000 personnel.[8] Currently the three divisions are each responsible for rapidly fielding a MAB when needed.

No account of the Corps would be complete without discussion of the unique place and role of Marine Aviation. The Marines have zealously guarded their right to possess their "own" air force. And no wonder -- Marines on the ground would be slaughtered without Marine air support. True, the Corps does possess some artillery and tanks but not nearly enough. Airpower thus compensates for the paucity of armor and cannon. To be effective in such circumstances, moreover, air support must be immediately responsive and exceptionally accurate. Marine airmen are intensively trained to function in such a demanding role. The Marines are also unwilling to relinquish the responsibility for local air superiority to another air arm. Even momentary loss of such air control could seal the fate of Marines below.

The Marines are, of course, dependent upon helicopters for mobility, both for "vertical envelopment" in the attack and for movement within a theatre. Marine aviation includes 180 Boeing Vertol CH-46 medium lift and 128 Sikorsky CH-53 heavy lift helicopters in active service.

Marine airpower will be significantly improved as the AV-8B V/STOL fighter bomber enters service. The improved Harrier is specifically configured for maximum payload and performance in the close support role. Procurement of 33 CH-53Es will furnish much needed augmentation of heavy lift helicopters. The aging and worn CH-46s must eventually be replaced, very likely with a V/STOL assault transport patterned upon the Bell XV-15.

Deficiencies in ground firepower and mobility are being addressed. In the artillery, 105mm. howitzers are being supplanted by the new M-198 155mm. fieldpieces. The infantry battalions are in the throes of reorganization and rearmament. A heavy machine gun platoon, equipped with eight .50 caliber machine guns and eight 40mm. automatic grenade throwers, has been added to the weapons company.[9] The anti-armor platoon now is armed with 32 Dragon launchers, an increase from 24. At the squad level, each five man fire team will have one long range light machine gun, the Belgian FN "Minimi". As a result of these and other changes firepower of a Marine battalion will be increased by 25 percent.[10]

The Marine Corps will employ the LAV-25, manufactured by General Motors of Canada, and winner of the light armored vehicle competition. Indeed the first year's production of the LAV-25 will go entirely to the Marines. In Marine service LAV-25 will carry a fire team as well as the crew and 25mm. machine cannon. An assault gun version will be armed with a 75 or 90mm. gun and an anti-tank variant will carry TOW missile launchers. Other versions of the basic vehicle will be fitted out for mortars, air defense, command, recovery, and supply roles.[11]

The Marine Corps plans to organize three light armored assault battalions, one of which will be assigned to the MAB in readiness for Indian Ocean service and another earmarked for the MAB designated for operations in Norway.[12]

Each LAV battalion will be made up of three armored assault companies, a weapons company, and headquarters and service companies.[13] Fifteen 25mm. gunned APCs and nine assault gun vehicles will be in each of the three assault companies. The weapons company will comprise 15 anti-tank vehicles, ten air defense cars, and six APCs. Counting all other types, command, recovery, supply, etc., a LAV battalion will number 145 cars.

Considerable debate has erupted within the Corps over the organization of the new light armor. The proposed LAV battalion is criticized as too large and unwieldy. Voices are raised to urge smaller, more efficient and more readily deployable LAV units.[14] Savings in manpower could be employed to form additional contingents to reinforce more infantry battalions.

Amid the furor over weaponry it is easy to lose sight of a less spectacular but no less essential item of equipment, the radio. In view of the high degree of Marine dependence upon quick air support radio communication is of particular significance. Soviet interception and jamming equipment is now ubiquitous the world over. The Marine Corps badly needs large quantities of new and electronically secure voice and data communications equipment.

Marines come ashore by helicopter and, of course, by amphibious assault across the beaches. The LVTP-7 is the amphibious assault vehicle in service with the Marine Corps. Propelled in water by water jet pumps, the LVTP-7A1 carries 25 troops. On land, the vehicle can attain a top speed of 43.2 miles per hour, has a road range of 288 miles, and is surprisingly agile.[15] The improved A1 model is now entering service. It is, however, lightly armed with a turret mounted .50 caliber machine gun. Its sheer bulkiness makes it an ideal target for every weapon imaginable.

Clearly the Marines need a far more effective assault vehicle than either the amphibian or the slow transport helicopter. It is precisely this need that can be brilliantly fulfilled by the air cushion landing craft. Air cushion vehicles have been pioneered and employed effectively in action by the British, particularly in the campaign fought in Borneo. Since 1971, the Soviet Union has brought air cushion vehicles into service for its naval infantry and can now boast the largest ACVs in the world, the 220 ton Aist class.

During the 1970s, prototype ACVs were built by Aerojet General and Bell Aerospace Textron to U.S. Navy specifications and thoroughly tested. The USMC has been eagerly seeking procurement of these LCACs (Landing Craft, Air Cushion), as they are officially designated. Finally, a production contract was issued to Bell early in 1982. Three LCACs will be built in fiscal year 1982, another three constructed in fiscal year 1983, six in fiscal year 1984, and twelve per year thereafter.[16] It is hoped that 107 LCACs will be brought into service.[17]

Powered by gas turbine engines, the LCAC can carry a 60 ton payload 200 nautical miles at a cruising speed of 60 miles per hour.[18] Even operating in 100 degree conditions and a 25 knot headwind, the LCAC can still cruise at 48 miles per hour.[19] On land sand dunes ten feet high can be readily surmounted.

The air cushion vehicle represents a quantum leap forward in amphibious assault strategy. A vast increase in speed and range of amphibious warfare is made possible by the LCAC. ACVs can be launched at considerable distances from shore and the vulnerability of amphibious shipping to enemy weaponry can thus be reduced.

The most significant strategic advance, however, is that LCACs can put Marines ashore on more than 70 percent of the coastlines of the world.[20] In contrast, lumbering barges are limited by shallow waters to some 17 percent of world's shores. Nor are LCACs constricted by considerations of beach structure, wave height, and tide. Moreover, shallow waters are characteristic of the Indian Ocean littoral. Air cushion vehicles are thus particularly needed for amphibious operations in this crucial arena.

Marines and their equipment must be deployed and supported by amphibious warfare ships. In 1967 the U.S. Navy numbered 162 amphibious ships in its ranks. The number of such ships has sharply declined until, in 1981, only 61 amphibious units were to be found in active service.[21] In the decade of the 1990s, all but six of the ships currently in service will be retired.[22] It will be necessary to build at least three ships each year over the next twenty years simply to maintain the present level of capability.[23]

The most immediate concern, however, is to build replacements for the Thomaston class of dock landing ships, all eight of which should be retired between 1984 and 1987. The first of an anticipated ten units in the LSD-41 class is now under construction and should join the fleet in 1984.[24] The first ship specifically designed to carry and repair LCACs, the Whidbey Island will weigh 15,726 tons at full load and will carry four LCACs, 440 troops, and their vehicles and supplies.[25] Whidbey Island will be equipped with electronic countermeasures gear and chaff dispensers for air defense and will be armed with two Phalanx multibarrel anti-aircraft 20mm. machine cannon.

Largest and most modern of the amphibious warfare ships now in service are the Tarawa class, five of which joined the fleet in the course of the late 1970s. A multipurpose assault transport, the Tarawa weighs 39,300 tons fully loaded and can make 24 knots.[26] As many as 2,500 troops can be accommodated. A well deck can carry four landing craft or two LCACs. The aviation complement offers a range of choices: 19 CH-53 heavy lift helicopters, 30 CH-46 medium lift helicopters, or 20 AV-8A fighter bombers. Air defense weapons include three dual purpose 5 inch cannon, six 20mm. guns, and two multiple Sea Sparrow missile launchers. The Tarawa is extremely sophisticated electronically, with a full range of communications and command equipment.

Replacements, however, will eventually have to be built for the Iwo Jima class of helicopter assault carriers, seven of which were delivered to the Navy during the 1960s. Now in the process of design is the LHD-1, an order for the first of this class could materialize in 1984.[27] It will serve the dual roles of amphibious assault and sea control. Helicopters and three LCACs will be carried in the assault mission. The LHD-1 will be specifically designed to support, command, and control operations of the new AV-8B at sea.[28]

Marines thus play a key role among U.S. rapidly deployable forces. Swift arrival of Marine Corps units in time of need is counted upon in three vital arenas. Arms and supplies are stockpiled in central Norway for a Marine Amphibious Brigade. U.S. Marines would join 6,000 Canadian troops and British Marines to help the Norwegians defend their country. Winter trained Canadian and British soldiers would fight inland while U.S. Marines operated along the coastline to prevent Soviet amphibious outflanking of Allied defense. In northern waters, strategically crucial Iceland may also need to be rescued in the event of Soviet attack.

Marine forces stationed in Hawaii, Okinawa, and bases in Japan sustain operations in the Pacific. Two Marine Amphibious Units are rotated in deployment with the fleet in the Indian Ocean.

Weapons, equipment, and supplies for a Marine Amphibious Brigade are pre-positioned in anchored ships at Diego Garcia in the Indian Ocean. The MAB earmarked for the Southwest Asian theatre trains intensively in desert and mechanized warfare in the arid wastelands of southern California.

Marine Amphibious Brigades are substantial formations; with integrated air support by helicopters and warplanes, and backed by service and support units and personnel. Present Marine commitments and combat forces may be as much as can realistically be expected of the Corps.

In sum, the Marine Corps possesses unique organization and capabilities, particularly relevant in the rapid deployment role and of major significance in a number of key theatres. However, the Corps should not be made over into a copy of the U.S. Army. Light armored vehicles, LCACs, AV-8Bs, and secure communications equipment can make it possible for the Marine Corps to remain viable in the combat operations it is so superbly fitted to perform.

94

1. Record, pp. 70-73; William S. Lind, "Defining Maneuver Warfare for the Marine Corps," *Marine Corps Gazette*, March 1980, pp. 55-58; and Gordon, p. 455.

2. Benjamin F. Schemmer, "Marine Amphibious Assault Forces Get Big Boost in New Defense Plan," *Armed Forces Journal International*, April 1982, p. 78.

3. Ibid.

4. Ibid.

5. Dov S. Zakheim, *The Marine Corps in the 1980's: Prestocking Proposals, the Rapid Deployment Force, and Other Issues* (Washington, D.C.: Congressional Budget Office, May 1980), p. 1.

6. The International Institute for Strategic Studies, *The Military Balance 1982-1983*, p. 8.

7. Ramon Lopez, "The United States Marine Corps in the 1980s," *International Defense Review*, April 1981, p. 435.

8. Zakheim, p. 12.

9. "More Changes to Infantry Battalion Structure," *Marine Corps Gazette*, January 1982, p. 25.

10. Ibid.

11. "US Marine Corps organizes LAV battalions," *International Defense Review*, February 1982, p. 191.

12. Ibid.

13. Ibid.

14. Captain Edwin W. Besch, USMC, "Light armored vehicles - uses and organizations," *Marine Corps Gazette*, January 1981, pp. 60-61.

15. R.M. Ogorkiewicz, "LVTP-7A1: the latest tracked landing vehicle," *International Defense Review*, April 1981, p. 466.

16. "Progress Being Made With LCACs," *Marine Corps Gazette*, October 1981, p. 4.

17. Ibid.

18. Labayle Couhat, p. 772.

19. "Progress Being Made With LCACs."

20. Benjamin F. Schemmer, "LCAC Contract Finally Lets USMC Put World War II Tactics Behind," <u>Armed Forces Journal International</u>, April 1982, p. 80.

21. Commander C.B. Peterson, USN, "LSD-41 Under Construction," <u>Marine Corps Gazette</u>, October 1981, p. 18.

22. Colonel John G. Miller, USA, "LCACs and the Lift Dilemma," <u>Marine Corps Gazette</u>, December 1981, p. 48.

23. Ibid.

24. Peterson. pp. 18-19.

25. Labayle Couhat, pp. 768-769.

26. Ibid., p. 765.

27. Mark Hewish, "US Navy League 1982 - weapon systems proliferate," <u>International Defense Review</u>, June 1982, p. 794.

28. Ibid.

X
Strategic Mobility:
Airlift and Sealift

The U.S. military shortcoming most fraught with serious consequence for the future is the lack of sufficient air and sea transport needed to deploy and support U.S. troops in major arenas around the world. The vast distances U.S. forces must traverse to reach areas vital to U.S. interests are daunting indeed. It is some 7,000 nautical miles by air from the continental United States to the Persian Gulf and approximately 12,000 nautical miles by sea around the Cape of Good Hope. To be sure, U.S. forces are stationed overseas in such key areas as West Germany, England, Korea, and Okinawa. Stockpiles of heavy weaponry, fuel, ammunition, and other supplies are pre-positioned in West Germany, Norway, Diego Garcia, and elsewhere. But such stockpiling is expensive (two sets of equipment at home and abroad for the same unit), entails considerable maintenance, and can be quite vulnerable to air attack. Nor can U.S. soldiers be stationed in every place they may be needed. Societies tenaciously guarding traditional values and lifestyles are understandably opposed to the presence of large bodies of foreign soldiery in their midst. Even where U.S. troops are in position overseas, substantial reinforcements must be forthcoming in time of crisis or conflict. Modern war consumes supplies in staggering quantities. A conflict of any duration and dimension can only be sustained by seaborne transport of fuel, ammunition, and weapons. Pre-positioning of supplies and commitment of U.S. forces overseas is thus essential but falls short of meeting the strategic needs of the United States. Hence the crucial need for U.S. airlift and sealift.

The relationship between air and sea transport is complex. Air transportation must be employed to get to far corners of the world quickly. Time frequently is critical, a battalion today is worth more than a brigade a week later. But ships can carry far more cargo more efficiently than can aircraft. Moreover

97

ships can transport bulky, large weaponry far more effectively. The dilemma is well illustrated by the U.S. resupply of Israel during the Yom Kippur War. More than 22,000 tons of supplies were airlifted to Israel. However the first ship to arrive carried more bulky cargo than did the entire airlift -- but, by that time the war was over.[1] Neither air nor sea transport alone will suffice, both are needed.

How much airlift does the United States need? At the express behest of Congress, the Joint Chiefs of Staff undertook in 1980-81 a thirteen month exhaustive study of airlift requirements. The Congressionally Mandated Mobility Study took into account pre-positioned stockpiles abroad and the eventual contribution of sealift. The Study concluded that U.S. needs demanded an airlift capability of 63 million ton miles/day.[2] What is our current capacity? According to the Study, U.S. airlift should be able to move 38 million ton miles/day.[3] The CMMS was based upon an array of modifications to transports to improve capability. Even so, the shortfall of 25 million ton miles/day is indeed significant.

Moreover, the CMMS asserted that 10 million ton miles/day of the airlift shortfall impacted upon bulky cargo -- the helicopters and armored vehicles so necessary to helicopter and mechanized formations.[4] According to CMMS, 24,740 tons of outsize equipment would be needed in the event of a conflict in the Persian Gulf; current delivery would fall short of meeting that requirement by 28 percent.[5]

The United States Air Force Military Airlift Command can draw upon a fleet of 77 Lockheed C-5As, 276 Lockheed C-141Bs, 67 Boeing 747s from the Civil Reserve Air Fleet, and 16 McDonnell Douglas KC-10 tankers from the Strategic Air Command.[6] Badly needed and long overdue spare parts have finally been funded for MAC, after some years of neglect. Because of long lead times for production, however, all the needed items will not be secured until fiscal year 1986.[7]

Backbone of U.S. strategic airlift is the Lockheed C-141B Starlifter. Capable of a range with maximum payload of 4,000 miles, the Starlifter can carry some 200 troops or 50 tons of cargo.[8] Such payloads represent a 30 percent increase made possible by lengthening the fuselage, a modification of the fleet completed in June 1982. An extremely valuable refueling in air capability has also been incorporated. So transformed, the C-141B represents the equivalent of 90 new transports at 1963 prices.[9] Although the modified Starlifter is a fine and much improved aircraft, it cannot handle outsize items.

The Lockheed C-5A Galaxy was designed to carry helicopters, tanks, self-propelled cannon, and other large and odd shaped cargo. The Galaxy can carry a

56.3 ton load over a range of 6,529 miles.[10] It is
fitted for refueling in air. Although the C-5 is a
giant aircraft, its landing gear permit it to fly in
and out of unpaved and soft airstrips. Loading and
unloading can be done simultaneously by front and rear
ramps.

Intense controversy has swirled around the C-5A.
Massive cost over-runs and other difficulties reduced
planned procurement from 200 to 81 aircraft. Wing
deficiencies have haunted the Galaxy and slashed wing
life to some 7,100 flying hours.[11] The wings are now
being rebuilt to a service life of an additional 30,000
flying hours, this program should be completed in
1986.[12] Strengthening of the wings and other
engineering improvements will increase the Galaxy's
cargo capacity by 25 percent.[13] However the sheer size
of the Galaxy does restrict operation to airfields with
wide parking ramps and taxi ways, it takes 150 feet to
turn the giant around.

Airlift can be augmented with planes drawn from the
Civil Reserve Air Fleet. Command exercises simulating
mobilization are held from time to time by MAC. Most
useful are some 67 Boeing 747 equivalents. Converted
to a freighter, the 747 can carry more cargo pallets
than a C-5, 50 and 36 respectively.[14] Or the 747 can
carry light trucks; ten 2 1/2 ton vehicles plus nine
jeeps. This cargo can be flown from the east coast of
the United States to the Persian Gulf non-stop.

But the 747 cannot accomodate outsize loads. It
needs thick concrete runways. High lift loading
machines are also required to handle the cargo.

The McDonnell Douglas KC-10A Extender, in service
with the Strategic Air Command, is a multi-purpose
tanker. On a deployment from the United States to
Europe, the Extender can refuel four fighter aircraft
and at the same time carry their maintenance crews and
support equipment, 15 tons of cargo.[15] The KC-10A will
thus be especially valuable in the rapid deployment of
fighter squadrons. If available in some numbers,
Extenders could enhance utilization of the C-5
considerably. The KC-10A is the only U.S. tanker that
is fitted to refuel both Air Force and Navy and Marine
aircraft.[16] This makes the KC-10A a particularly
important plane in the Persian Gulf where warplanes
from all U.S. services must fly and fight together.

Late in 1981 the Air Force announced the winner of
a contest to design a new transport capable of carrying
outsize cargo from the United States directly to small
airstrips close to actual battle zones. McDonnell
Douglas emerged victorious in the competition. The
C-17 incorporates new technology in high lift and short
takeoff features. It will fly in and out of soft
airstrips 90 feet wide and only 3,000 feet long.[17] A
maximum payload of 86 tons will be carried. The range

can be augmented through refueling in air.

Flight tests of the C-17 would commence late in 1986. Full scale production could be anticipated in the late 1980s. The fate of the C-17, however, depends upon Congressional funding. In any case, the C-17 is too late a development to remedy the immediate and pressing lack of enough airlift now.

Confronted with an urgent need for a substantial increase in airlift as soon as possible, the U.S. Air Force turned to the existing C-5 and KC-10 production lines. MAC will secure an additional 50 Galaxies and 44 KC-10As. Thirty two more Boeing 747 equivalents will be added to the Civil Reserve Air Fleet.[18] The Lockheed C-5B will incorporate the engineering modifications presently included in the rebuilt C-5As. KC-10As will be quite valuable for many purposes and will be readily available from a current production line.

The C5B/KC-10A procurement decision touched off a spectacular display of political fireworks in Congress. Boeing proposed the purchase of 50 747Fs, in place of the Lockheed C-5Bs, for the Military Airlift Command. Corporate rivalries and political passions were inflamed by the impact of severe recession and Congressional elections in the fall of 1982. Finally, Congress did approve the C-5B/KC-10A program in August of 1982. Unhappily, airlift concerns in the future could be complicated by the reservoir of ill will left in the wake of this affair.

Acquisition of the new C-5Bs and KC-10As and the 747 increment to CRAF will increase airlift a total of eighteen million ton miles/day.[19] Outsize cargo capability will be augmented by eight million ton miles/day. Requirements of outsize cargo for the Persian Gulf scenario delineated by the CMMS will thus be fulfilled.[20]

Although the airlift shortfall will be substantially reduced, air transport capability will remain seven million ton miles/day below the requirement established by the CMMS. Moreover, should crises erupt in NATO Europe and the Persian Gulf simultaneously, airlift of outsize cargo could fall short by as much as 66 percent.[21] C-141Bs remain dependent on long concrete runways. Even though C-5s can use rough fields, airstrips must be wide and long. So airlift needs remain to be fully addressed.

In the first days of any conflict airlift is crucial. Following the initial stages of a conflict sealift is essential. No fighting can be sustained without sea transportation. The Military Sealift Command reports that 90 percent of the supplies needed to sustain U.S. troops in combat must be conveyed by sea.[22]

The present deplorable -- and perilous -- state of

U.S. sealift is incisively summarized by John M. Collins:

> Sealift has gotten short shrift for more than 30 years. Interest in the 1960s centered on quick reaction instead of sustained support, but few funds were forthcoming for forces afloat, even for that purpose. Consequently, U.S. assets, which reached their apogee during World War II, have been on a down-hill slide for three decades. . . .
>
> The conversion has been from many ships to few; from military ships to civilian ships; from U.S. ships to foreign flags; from general cargo to container ships; from small, adaptable ships to large ones whose applications are limited. Our 'mothball' fleet, which once served well, is mainly scrap.[23]

The Military Sealift Command of the U.S. Navy directly owned or chartered 29 cargo ships and 31 tankers in 1981.[24]. Such a small nucleus must, of course, be much augmented in time of emergency.

MSC must thus rely upon the "mothball" fleet, the National Defense Reserve Fleet maintained by the Maritime Administration. The NRDF in January 1981 numbered 163 dry cargo ships, 129 of which were Victory ships from the Second World War.[25] Victory ships can carry a variety of outsize items and are self-loading, but are small, slow, old, and often dilapidated. To reach the Indian Ocean from a west coast port, a Victory ship will require eight and a half days more than a modern C-4 ship. To bring these freighters into service would take time, since many would need repair, and in any case crews would have to be assembled for them. Indeed, eight months may be needed to make all the fleet serviceable.[26]

A Ready Reserve Force of the most modern ships in the NDRF has been especially prepared to be swiftly available. In 1982 the RRF numbered 28 ships.[27] These selected ships are "igloo" sealed in dehumidified storage, and can be readied for service in five to ten days. But crews must be hastily brought together before these ships can put to sea.

Can the U.S. Merchant Marine be tapped? The Sealift Readiness Program does commit 207 active merchant ships to meet military needs in an emergency.[28] But these ships are engaged in carrying minerals and raw materials to U.S. factories and thus cannot readily be diverted from that vital task without risking the collapse of the U.S. industrial economy. Moreover, the break-bulk freighter, readily adaptable

to military cargo, is rapidly disappearing, supplanted
by the much more profitable container ship. But the
container ship is not at all suited to carry vehicles.
It does not possess onboard gantry cranes for loading
and unloading, being dependent on port facilities for
that purpose.

To be sure, the entire U.S. Merchant Marine could
be pressed into service if a dire emergency arose.
But, suffering from dangerous neglect, the U.S.
merchant fleet has fallen, as of April 1982, to a low
of 575 ocean going ships.[29] Indeed, less than four
percent of U.S. dry cargo is shipped in U.S. flag
ships.[30]

True, there are some 312 U.S. owned ships operating
under foreign flags of convenience.[31] All but 16,
however, are container ships or large tankers.
Predominantly alien crews might well balk at service in
war zones.

What programs are underway to augment sealift? The
maritime prepositioning force at Diego Garcia has been
immensely strengthened, six units have joined the
original group of seven. The increased store of
supplies doubles the length of time one MAB can fight
and supports Army and Air Force units as well. As more
ships come into service, supplies will be stocked in
Southwest Asia sufficient to support considerably
greater U.S. forces, perhaps the equivalent of three
MABs.

Some twelve to fifteen ships are being purchased or
leased by MSC for use or conversion as vehicle
transports. Such a policy is made possible by
recession and the depressed state of international
commerce. When State Lines, Inc. went bankrupt, MSC
was able to secure four large vehicle cargo ships.
Designated the Maine class these ships weigh 33,765
tons fully loaded and can sustain a cruising speed of
23 knots. They can accommodate vehicle, container, and
liquid cargo and can operate helicopters amidships.

Another windfall occurred when eight very large and
fast freighters became available from Sea-Land, Inc.
Built in the Netherlands and West Germany, these ships
weigh 51,795 tons at full load and can make 33 knots.[33]
The SL-7s will be converted to "roll-on, roll-off"
configuration, equipped with ramps, deck cranes, and
helicopter landing areas. Anti-aircraft and
anti-missile defense will also be featured, for this
purpose the British Seawolf is being considered. It is
anticipated that the conversion program will be
completed by July 1985.[34]

This fleet of SL-7s will be able to carry all the
equipment and much of the service and support of a
heavy mechanized division. Sailing from the east coast
of the United States and rounding the Cape of Good
Hope, the SL-7s can deliver the mechanized division to

Southwest Asia in 17 days.[35] No wonder the commander of MSC terms the SL-7 the "cornerstone of our Fast Sealift package."[36]

Clearly the United States is scrambling to lay hands on as many suitable ships as possible. But the dearth of cargo ships needed to sustain U.S. overseas deployments will not be easily overcome. In many ways the United States is paying the high price exacted by neglect of the U.S Merchant Marine.

1. Collins, pp. 270-271.

2. Clarence A. Robinson, Jr., "USAF Seeks Continued Effort on C-17," Aviation Week & Space Technology, 1 February 1982, p. 24.

3. Ibid.

4. Ibid., p. 25.

5. Benjamin F. Schemmer, "Budget Cutters Are Only Ones Likely to Win Battle Over C-5B/747F/C-17 Airlift Alternatives," Armed Forces Journal International, July 1982, p. 48.

6. Robinson, Jr., "USAF Seeks Continued Effort of C-17."

7. Luanne K. Levens and Benjamin F. Schemmer, Interview with General James R. Allen, USAF, Armed Forces Journal International, July 1982, p. 54.

8. Gunston, pp. 227-228.

9. Schemmer, "Budget Cutters Are Only Ones Likely to Win Battle Over C-5B/747F/C-17 Airlift Alternatives," p. 42.

10. Gunston, p. 222.

11. Collins, p. 273.

12. Bates, p. 27.

13. Robinson, Jr., "USAF Seeks Continued Effort on C-17."

14. Schemmer, "Budget Cutters Are Only Ones Likely to Win Battle Over C-5B/747F/C-17 Airlift Alternatives," p. 43.

15. Collins, p. 273.

16. "KC-10A: US Air Mobility Boost," Air International, October 1980, p. 169.

17. "McDonnell Douglas Gets Nod to Build C-X," Armed Forces Journal International, October 1981, p. 20.

18. Robinson, Jr., "USAF Seeks Continued Effort on C-17," p. 24.

19. Ibid.

20. Schemmer, "Budget Cutters Are Only Ones Likely to Win Battle Over C-5B/747F/C-17 Airlift Alternatives," p. 48.

21. Ibid.

22. Kyle.

23. Collins, p. 277.

24. Bates, p. 27.

25. Deborah M. Kyle, "US Sealift: Dwindling Resources vs. Rising Need?," <u>Armed Forces Journal International</u>, May 1981, p. 37, and Collins, p. 281.

26. Collins, p. 282.

27. Kyle, "Sealift.§

28. Kyle, "US Sealift: Dwindling Resources vs. Rising Need?"

29. Kyle, "Sealift.§

30. Ibid., p. 58.

31. Collins.

32. Labayle Couhat, p. 806.

33. Ibid., p. 804.

34. Hewish, p. 794.

35. Kyle, "Sealift," p. 60.

36. Ibid., p. 58.

XI
The U.S. Navy and
the Super Carrier

An immense increase in United States naval power constitutes the centerpiece of the Reagan administration's military program. Envisioned in the 1983-1987 five year shipbuilding plan is an awesome buildup of United States' strength at sea. During this period, the U.S. Navy seeks the funds to build 133 new ships and submarines, some 60 of which would be major warships.[1] In addition, 16 old ships will be reactivated or undergo conversion or overhaul.[2] The long run goal of this sweeping program is a 600 ship fleet designed to assure maritime supremacy in every ocean of the world. To achieve such an objective it will be necessary to begin construction of some 26 ships each year.

In Fiscal Year 1983, the Navy called for funds to start 18 new ships and submarines and seven conversions -- and won Congressional authorization for all save one Trident submarine.[3] Of the ten most costly weapons programs, no less than five are Navy, four of them warships and attack submarines.[4]

The heart of the U.S. surface fleet will, it is hoped, be 15 super carrier battle groups, including six nuclear fueled Nimitz class carriers. The Navy hopes to fund the purchase of 1,953 new aircraft during the Five year Plan. This will cost some 47 billion dollars.[5] A 13th carrier air wing will form in 1983 and it is hoped a 14th air wing can be operational in 1987. Warplane production for the Navy is anticipated to rise to almost 400 aircraft in Fiscal Year 1985 and 442 by Fiscal Year 1987.[6] Aircraft currently in service will be extensively modified to improve capabilities and extend operational life.

To distribute naval offensive striking power Tomahawk cruise missiles will be widely deployed. The Navy plans to equip some 150 surface warships and submarines with 2,600 launchers and 3,994 Tomahawk cruise missiles.[7] Employment of the Harpoon anti-ship missile, already operational in 1982 with 120 ships, 36 attack submarines, and 76 Orion patrol planes, will be expanded to 3,000 missiles.[8]

To augment naval power projection and free carriers for urgent missions it is hoped to reactivate the four Iowa class battleships. In addition to their sixteen inch gun batteries the Iowas will be armed with Harpoon and Tomahawk missiles.[9] Refurbishing the battleships is less costly and less time consuming than constructing new counterparts.

But older warships are not always amenable to conversion. New Jersey and Iowa will return to service. But much equipment was removed from Wisconsin, which was also severely damaged by fire. The keel of the Missouri was badly strained by grounding and her speed is consequently sharply restricted.

The Navy had also envisioned a swift increase in airpower at sea through recommissioning the older carriers Oriskany and Bon Homme Richard. Regrettably, the internal dimensions of Oriskany preclude operating AV-8 V/STOL fighter bombers and constrict the ship to A-4 and A-7 light attack aircraft. Bon Homme Richard is in better condition than her sister, a new flight deck was installed and an overhaul completed before retirement to reserve. Equipped with new A-18s, the Bon Homme Richard might well rejoin the fleet.

Submarines are not neglected in the Navy's Five Year Plan. Funding for 17 nuclear fueled Los Angeles class attack submarines is to be secured.[10] Eight former Polaris SSBN boats will be refitted for the attack role. A force of 100 nuclear fueled attack submarines, at a minimum, is the goal of the Navy.[11]

Virtually all attack submarines will eventually be armed with Harpoon missiles. The Los Angeles class will carry twelve vertical launch tubes for Tomahawk missiles.[12] Inasmuch as surface warships are quite vulnerable to the submarine, U.S. attack submarines will be needed to protect the super carrier from its Soviet underwater nemesis.

The cost of this sweeping program will not be light. Excluding strategic SSBN Trident submarines from consideration and calculating shipbuilding costs for general purpose naval ships, Douglas Mitchell estimates the Navy's five year program will cost 122 billion dollars in constant Fiscal Year 1982 dollars.[13] If inflation at an annual rate of five percent is factored in, the estimate rises to 133.6 billion dollars.[14] Moreover, as already indicated, the price tag for more than 1,900 new aircraft and modification of warplanes currently in service is almost 50 billion dollars.

Nor can the cost of expanding the Navy be spread out over a longer time frame. Many ships now in service will be worn out in the 1990s and need to be replaced. If funding for a 600 ship fleet is planned on a ten year basis, estimated costs rise to 183.6 billion dollars, 234.9 billion dollars if five percent inflation is assumed.[15]

These figures do not take into account the cost of the maintenance, fuel, ammunition, and crew needed to operate the fleet. To operate a 600 ship Navy Michael MccGwire claculates that annual naval appropriations of 14.4 billion dollars (in Fiscal Year 1983 dollars) will be required.[16] Inflation, of course, will increase this sum. Such appropriations would be double the average funding secured in the past fifteen years.[17]

What drives the cost of general purpose surface fleet expansion? The super carrier is the capital ship of the U.S. Navy. Expensive as they are, the super carriers are but a segment of the price to be paid for a carrier battle group. Each carrier must be protected by six heavily armed and highly sophisticated escort cruisers and destroyers. Such a super carrier battle group costs 17 billion dollars.[18] Indeed, Douglas Mitchell emphasizes that, for every dollar spent on a super carrier, an additional $7.10 must be expended on escort ships and their electronics and weaponry,[19]

These calculations omit the cost of the necessary attack submarine escort of the CBG, such a submarine costs some 670 million dollars. Nor do these figures take into account the land based Air Force F-15 fighter squadrons that may be required to help protect the super carrier.

Why does the U.S. Navy need 15 super carriers? The demand for these warships is founded upon an interlocking set of key assumptions.

Under normal peacetime circumstances, one third of the carriers, escort units, and support ships are on station at any given time. Others are being resupplied, undergoing routine maintenance or in short overhaul. Frequent rotation affords time at home for crew members, a vital element in morale.

For a number of years U.S. carrier forces have been forward deployed in the Mediterranean Sea and in the western Pacific. Forces near at hand where need may arise have been deemed more potent than warships homeported far away in the United States. Valuable training is afforded by the continuous operations entailed by forward deployment. Forces in place can act as a stabilizing deterrent, preventing crises erupting.

The Navy strongly emphasizes the value of the two carrier group. Charles D. Allen, Jr. puts the argument, noting that a one carrier deployment:

> . . . resulting capability, compared with that of a two-carrier battle group, is well below half, and perhaps closer to one-fourth.

> Single-carrier groups cannot conduct
> round-the-clock combat operations for more
> than a day or so because of crew fatigue, and
> they lack the number of aircraft necessary to
> provide defense in depth against a heavy
> attack from more than one sector.[20]

In accord with this viewpoint, it has been the
practice of the United States to commit two carrier
battle groups in the Mediterranean and the western
Pacific. For these deployments twelve carriers
suffice. But the crises in the Indian Ocean compelled
the United States to bring two carriers into that
arena. Perforce U.S. deployments in the Mediterranean
and the Pacific were drawn down and weakened. Above
all, morale suffered from extraordinarily protracted
duty with the fleet in the Indian Ocean. Not a few
naval careers were abruptly terminated when a man was
confronted by his wife with the choice: "the carrier
or me!"

Predicated on these assumptions, 15 carriers and
four battleships would permit the U.S. Navy to rotate
two carriers to the Mediterranean, two carriers to the
western Pacific, and one carrier and a battleship to
the Indian Ocean. Another battleship might be
stationed in the Caribbean.

In the event of war with the Soviet Union, the U.S.
Navy plans to unleash carrier airpower against air and
naval bases in the Soviet Union. Conflict with the
Soviet Union, in Navy opinion, will escalate swiftly to
engulf the world. In such circumstances everything
that floats will be hurled into the fray.

The super carrier is the heart and soul of the
U.S. surface fleet. The giant attack carrier is indeed
a formidable weapon. As a number of studies have
concluded, the super carrier profits from economy of
scale and carries a large and balanced air contingent
and immense quantities of ammunition and fuel.[21] High
speed and long range are attractive features of the
super carrier. Nimitz and her escorts, for example,
averaged twenty five knots traveling 11,000 miles from
the Mediterranean around the Cape of Good Hope to the
Indian Ocean.[22] Norman Friedman sums up the case for
the super carrier:

> Thus it can be argued that, for a given level
> of capability well beyond the capacity of any
> small carrier, the equivalent force of large
> carriers will be less expensive to operate,
> harder to locate (at least as far as infrared
> and radar signatures are concerned) and also
> harder to sink.[23]

In 1982 twelve super carriers were in active

service with the U.S. fleet. In 1983 the Carl Vinson, a nuclear fueled carrier of the Nimitz class, will become operational. The Theodore Roosevelt, an Improved Nimitz class, will join the carrier fleet in 1987. Whether the Bon Homme Richard can be reactivated remains to be seen. In the early 1990s the older Midway and Coral Sea must be retired. To replace the Midway class the Navy requested, in the Fiscal Year 1983 budget, funds for the eventual construction of two Improved Nimitz carriers. Although Congressional authorization was secured, looming huge federal budget deficits may delay funding for the two super carriers.

An excellent example of the super carrier is to be seen in the nuclear fueled Nimitz class. Weighing 96,351 tons at full load, the Nimitz is built of high tensile, extraordinarily strong steel; and features more than 2,000 compartments, foam equipment for fire suppression, and an elaborate pumping system.[24] Nimitz carries 1,954 tons of aircraft munitions and enough warplane fuel for 16 days of intensive operations.[25] An array of highly sophisticated electronic installations is featured; radars, countermeasures gear, satellite communications, automatic data transmission links, and a tactical data system which instantly presents the commander with a picture of a given tactical situation.

A super carrier is protected by 24 F-4 or F-14 fighters which work hand in hand with four airborne early warning E-2C aircraft.[26] Antisubmarine defense is entrusted to ten S-3A planes and six SH-3 helicopters. Twenty four A-7E machines fly light attack missions. Long range all weather attack is the responsibility of ten A-6Es supported by four EA-6B electronic countermeasures planes and four KA-6D tankers. Reconnaissance is flown by three modified F-14s.

It is clear, however, that half the aircraft must be devoted to defense of the carrier and its escorts. All the costly resources of a carrier battle group are dedicated to support a strike capability of 34 attack planes. Obviously, carrier aviation serves another -- and perhaps even more important -- purpose, it can shield amphibious assault groups and vital convoys.

Twelve carrier air wings constitute the front line of current U.S. naval airpower. Another wing will be formed in 1983 based on the Vinson. In 1987 a 14th air group will come into service with the Theodore Roosevelt.

The most crucially important warplane in the U.S. Navy is the Grumman F-14A long range interceptor. In a major decision in 1982, the Navy selected the F-14 as the chief fighter of the fleet.[27] No less than 845 F-14s will be purchased to replace the aging and obsolete F-4s.[28] Only the older and smaller Midway, unable to handle F-14s, will be furnished with McDonnell Douglas F-18s. Each large deck super carrier will be equiped with two squadrons of the F-14s.

Two interwoven factors weighed heavily in the selection of the F-14. Effective defense of carrier battle groups now demands that the outer defense zone be expanded to 500 nautical miles and only the F-14 could meet this imperative.[29] Second, sharply increasing numbers of Soviet Tu-26 attack bombers are being deployed and armed with a new long ranging air to surface cruise missile.[30] Only an improved F-14 could cope with this lethal challenge to the carrier.

Powered by twin turbofan engines, the "swingwing" F-14A carries a crew of two and was specifically designed for the long range interception and air superiority roles. The Tomcat is capable of 1,564 miles per hour.[31] Thanks to the automatic computer controlled variable geometry wings, the F-14 can hold its own as a dogfighter with companions of its generation such as the F-15 Eagle. Configured for the air combat patrol mission, Tomcat can spend forty eight minutes on station at a radius of 300 nautical miles.[32] If loiter time is reduced range can be considerably extended.

Powerful radar enables the F-14 to detect aircraft more than 170 nautical miles distant.[33] Even cruise missiles can be discerned some 65 nautical miles away. Twenty four targets can be tracked simultaneously and six long range Phoenix missiles launched against the most threatening of them.[34]

A complicated warplane, the F-14 is demanding and expensive to maintain. A number of Tomcats have fallen victim, during catapult launches, to afterburner blowout and engine stall. Both the F-14 and the Phoenix missile must be modified to cope with a heavy electronic countermeasures environment.

Many significant improvements are now being rapidly incorporated into both the F-14 and the Phoenix missile. Embodied in the AIM-54C version of the Phoenix are modifications that enhance accuracy, effectiveness against very low flying targets such as cruise missiles, and reliability.[35] Also moving into production are developments designed to frustrate ECCM against the Phoenix.[36]

In Fiscal Year 1984, the F-14C will come into production. The C model will include many new features.[37] A new computer and inertial navigation system will be installed. A tactical information system, resistant to ECM, will be another new feature. A medium pulse rate frequency radar will be less susceptible to ECM jamming. A threat warning system and self-protection jammer will also be fitted.

Beginning in Fiscal Year 1985, the F-14D will emerge from the production lines. The major feature of the D model will be the installation of new engines, either the Pratt and Whitney PW1130 or the General Electric F101 DFE, each capable of 27,400 lbs. static thrust with afterburning.[38]

The General Electric engines have already been tested in the F-14, and resulted in remarkable improvement in performance, range and handling qualities.[39] Engine stall is virtually eliminated in the F101. With the F101 the Tomcat can climb if need be, fully loaded, on one engine without using afterburner. Rapid throttle movement is possible under all conditions. The F-14/101 can spend an hour and a half on station at a radius of 300 nautical miles compared to forty eight minutes for the F-14A or range can be commensurately extended.[40] The F101 powered Tomcat also registers an impressive increase in acceleration.

It is clear that the full potential of the F-14 design has not yet been realized. A spacious and well formed airframe, the F-14 can accommodate many new electronic and avionic systems and weapons. A quantum increase in performance can flow from the installation of new engines and avionics. Fortunately, production of the F-14 can be swiftly expanded by Grumman.

Consideration should also be given to equipping the Tomcat for the attack role, paralleling the development of the F-15E Strike Eagle. Fitted with forward looking infrared radar, a laser designator, a double density computer, and a multiplex database, the F-14 could unleash Harpoon and Tomahawk missiles. Nor would the F-14 need a fighter escort, it would be more than capable of defending itself to and from a target.

The all weather, long range attack machine in current U.S. naval service is the Grumman A-6E. The A-6 has enjoyed a long career, being successively modernized with highly sophisticated electronic systems. A two seat, twin engine machine, the Intruder can carry a maximum payload of nine tons or, more typically, three tons of bombs can be carried over a range of 950 nautical miles.[41] In order to raise understrength squadrons from ten aircraft to twelve, the A-6 will continue in production through Fiscal Year 1987.[42]

Moreover, a number of new systems are being added to the A-6. An all weather stand-off attack system, utilizing synthetic aperture radar, will be installed.[43] Wiring and pylons are fitted enabling the Intruder to launch Walleye, Maverick, high speed antiradiation, and Harpoon missiles.

However the A-6 is a bomber and cannot double in the fighter role. Indeed, in situations where considerable fighter opposition must be confronted, the Intruder requires a fighter escort. Its survival hinges on bad weather, the cover of darkness, and its suite of electronic countermeasures.

A major new warplane program, the McDonnell Douglas F/A-18 Hornet, is engulfed in controversy. Originally, the Hornet was envisaged to be a multi-mission replacement for the A-7E light attack machine and for a large part of the aging F-4 fighter inventory.[44] The F/A-18 was also intended to succeed the A-4 attack planes and Phantom fighters in the Marine Corps aircraft inventory. Thus one airplane would replace three different machines in service, and economies in large scale production and in operation could be realized. It was also hoped that the Hornet would be a relatively low cost supplement to the F-14 Tomcat in the fighter role. To meet all these requirements, the largest navy warplane procurement program got underway with a goal of 1,366 aircraft.[45]

But development of the Hornet proved to be far more costly than had been foreseen. The cost of the F/A-18 project skyrocketed to become the most expensive of all Navy weapons programs in 1980.[46] The Navy decided to rely upon increased numbers of F-14s as the prime carrier fighter. In the dedicated fighter role the Hornet is thus relegated to the smaller Midway carrier and Marine aviation. Moreover, the Marines selected an improved V/STOL close support machine, the AV-8B, to fulfill their attack mission. If secured the Hornet may supplant only the A-7E on super carrier decks and the Phantom in Marine air service.

Indeed, during late summer and fall of 1982 the fate of the F/A-18 has hung in the balance. The Secretary of the Navy has threatened to cancel the Hornet program if the price was not substantially reduced.[47] In a rare display of major weapon price cutting, the unit cost of the Hornets purchased in Fiscal Year 1982 was slashed to 22.5 million dollars each.[48] More importantly, the manufacturers were compelled to accept a fundamental change in the contract to a fixed price contract. Under the new arrangement, the firms can no longer pass inflation increases on to the Navy.[49]

But a heavy blow fell upon the F/A-18 when the Navy's Air Test and Evaluation Squadrons, following weeks of operational testing, condemned the Hornet.[50] The official report from these squadrons opposes the Hornet in the attack role and states that it is not a suitable successor to the A-7E. It is argued that the Hornet does not possess the range and endurance needed to carry out the attack mission.

Fierce controversy now surrounds the F/A-18 program. If the larger program is now terminated, production will probably be halted after some 260 Hornets will have been procured. Thus the Hornet would only serve in the fighter squadrons of the Marine Corps and on the carrier Midway. Other countries have put in orders for the Hornet: 75 for Australia, 138 for Canada, and 84 for Spain. These nations may cancel their arrangements to secure F-18s and opt for other warplanes.

The Navy is caught in an unhappy set of dilemmas. The A-6 and A-7 aircraft are fine attack machines. But they are vulnerable to enemy fighters. Hardly a corner of the world remains where the Navy could not expect to encounter substantial fighter opposition. Hence A-6 and A-7 missions need F-14 fighter escort. But the F-14s are sorely needed to protect the carriers. The Navy can ill afford to spare F-14s for escort duties and thus put the carriers at risk. Now, the F/A-18 possesses neither the interceptor capabilities to defend carriers nor sufficient range to carry out the attack mission.

The Navy should seriously study the development of an attack version of the F-14. Certainly the F-14 is large enough to accommodate the array of electronics the attack role requires. General Electric engines can furnish the fuel economy, immense range, and handling qualities demanded by the attack mission. The increasing proliferation in the world of high performance fighter bombers and missile armed fast patrol boats now compels the carrier to operate farther away from enemy shores than has been true heretofore. An ever increasing premium will be placed upon range as a necessary attribute of carrier based airpower.

What is the major purpose the U.S. fleet is intended to serve? The U.S. Navy fulfills many important purposes but, like all the armed forces, it must be designed to function in the worst case situation -- war with the Soviet Union. What are the primary missions of the U.S. Navy in such a conflict? Key naval missions in a war with the Soviet Union are manifold; many, such as nuclear strategic, are entrusted to SSBN and attack submarines. What, then, will be the role of the surface fleet and the super carrier?

It must be emphasized that Navy leadership is not a single minded monolith. As John A. Williams points out:

In some respects there is not one U.S. Navy, but three, all wearing the same uniform: the surface navy, the air navy, and the submarine navy. Each competes for its preferred role in power projection. . . . The result is a naval posture which is . . . to some degree a consequence of bureaucratic infighting within the Navy itself, among participants whose positions are determined at least in part by narrow perspectives and self-interest.[51]

A powerful faction within the leadership of the U.S. Navy, strongly supported by Navy Secretary John F. Lehman, urges an offensive strategy based upon the super carrier battle group. This offensive strategy embraces three fundamental features.

"Horizontal escalation" would attempt to meet Soviet aggression in areas where we are at a disadvantage by widening the conflict and striking at points where the Russians are vulnerable. It is argued that U.S. and Soviet naval forces are so intermingled in the oceans of the world that geographic delimitation of a conflict at sea would be impossible. The United States must, so the argument goes, seize the initiative and sweep the Soviet surface Navy and merchant and fishing fleets from the seas.[52]

As a logical corollary of horizontal escalation, global conflict is held to entail "simultaneous" naval operations in all major sea theatres. This view also flows from the conviction that the very nature of warfare at sea is universal and can admit no clear lines of geographical demarcation. In order to carry out operations on so vast a scale an immense array of powerful -- and costly -- warships would be necessary.

But the heart and soul of the offensive strategy is an assault upon the naval and naval air base complexes in the Soviet Union, particularly the Kola Peninsula near Murmansk and the Vladivostok area in the Far East. Air attacks, with conventional weapons, would be unleashed from super carrier battle groups and the foe throttled in his lair. The assumptions undergirding this strategy are summarized by former Chief of Naval Operations, Admiral Thomas B. Hayward:

> We must fight on the terms which are most advantageous to us. This would require taking the war to the enemy's naval forces with the objective of achieving the earliest possible destruction of his capability to interfere with our use of the sea areas for support of our overseas forces and allies. In this sense sea control is an offensive rather than a defensive function. The prompt destruction of opposing naval forces is the most economical and effective means to assure control of the sea areas required for successful prosecution of the war and support of the U.S. and allied war economies. Our current offensive naval capabilities, centered on the carrier battle forces and their supporting units, are well-suited for the execution of this strategy.[53]

These major attacks would be mounted by three

carrier battle groups. Each CBG would include two super carriers, three Aegis air defense cruisers, five guided missile air defense cruisers and destroyers, and four anti-submarine destroyers. Nuclear fueled attack submarines would also support these battle groups. Indeed, U.S. attack submarines would be deployed well forward into the Norwegian Sea and the Northwest Pacific in the early stages of any conflict.

Is this super carrier centered offensive strategy feasible? Is is desirable?

Assuredly diplomatic efforts to contain a local or regional conflict and prevent the eruption of a wider war could be contradicted and even undercut by a naval strategy which places a premium on swift escalation on a global scale. The United States might fall into the role of aggressor, losing the support of U.S. and allied peoples and alienating public opinion around the world. Escalation, once unleashed, could be very difficult indeed to restrain or reverse. What might the U.S. reaction be to Soviet air attacks upon our air and naval bases in New England and the Pacific Northwest? The U.S. response to the Japanese attack on Pearl Harbor is a matter of historical record.

But success is not likely to crown super carrier assaults upon the homeland bastions of the Russian fleet. The only suitable aircraft would be the long range all weather A-6 attack plane. Even six carriers, however, carry a total of but 60 Intruders, supported by tanker and electronic countermeasures versions of the A-6. A modest force this is indeed, upon which so heavy a burden of decision must ride.

Moreover, the carrier cannot hide in the vastness of the oceans any longer. "Spy in the sky" space surveillance satellites track the path of warships on the high seas. Thus detected, long before they could strike at Russian bases, the carriers would be forced to run the gauntlet of Soviet defenses. Admiral Stansfield Turner, USN (ret.), and Captain George Thibault, USN and Chairman of the Department of Military Strategy at the National War College, outline the ordeal the carriers would suffer:

> By the time the carriers were within 1,600 miles of Soviet air bases, they would be within range of over 90 percent of the U.S.S.R.'s land-based bombers. Yet, the Soviet bases would still be over 1,000 miles beyond the range of carrier aircraft.

> Travelling at 25 knots for those last 1,000 miles, the carrier forces would be subject to Soviet air bombardment for nearly two days before it was close enough to strike Soviet bases. The force would also be subject to

attack by submarines and surface ships with long-range missiles that would have been deployed along the route. In short, we would be fighting the Soviets on their turf at times and places of their choosing, well before we could assume the offensive.[54]

Nor would Soviet missiles need to sink a super carrier in order to put it out of action. As Admiral Elmo R. Zumwalt, Jr., USN (ret.), points out:

If the Battle Group's aircraft carrier is not sunk but merely disabled, all of the offensive punch of the Battle Group disappears. No modern ship, including very large aircraft carriers, can perform all its missions after multiple cruise missile hits with conventional warheads, or one cruise missile near miss with nuclear warhead.[55]

Perhaps F-14 and F-15 fighters may be able to fend off Russian missile firing attack planes, but U.S. attack submarines could be overwhelmed by sheer numbers of Soviet cruise missile and attack submarines. In a total war situation, surface warships are quite vulnerable to submarine attack. U.S. naval exercises pitting U.S. submarines against carriers and their escorts have underlined carrier vulnerability repeatedly and painfully. Anthony H. Cordesman reports:

Several senior submariners note that during hunt-and-kill exercises in the Mediterranean, the nuclear submarines are assumed to have achieved a kill if they can fire a flare without detection, and that on some nights the end result has looked like a fireworks display. One U.S. submarine even had the nerve to surface during such exercises and ask its targets for more flares.[56]

Survival of U.S. carriers in a conflict with the Soviet Union may thus depend upon the issue of the duel beneath the sea.

Even so, the USSR could well be tempted to unleash ballistic missiles, ICBMs or IRBMs, upon U.S. carrier battle groups. The Russians possess more than enough ICBMs to spare. ICBM warheads are assuredly powerful enough to devastate a battle group. Moreover, such an ICBM attack upon a CBG would be a clearly defensive strike upon a military target, not an offensive nuclear assault upon the U.S. people and homeland. Thus does the carrier offensive strategy, directed at bases in the USSR, give added impetus to the escalatory thrust, tempting the superpowers to cross the nuclear threshold.

What if the nuclear threshold has already been breached? In a nuclear war situation, to dispatch carriers in a frontal assault upon the Soviet Union would be suicidal folly. What is to be done? Retired Admiral Thor Hansen puts the matter squarely, "Why in hell do you fly in an airplane to attack those bases when you can use a missile?"[57] Missiles, preferably launched from submarines, should be the primary offensive striking power of the U.S. Navy.

Preoccupation with the carrier offensive strategy overlooks and neglects other key and vital missions. Funds lavished upon the highly sophisticated super carrier and its escorts are funds denied to other programs and weapon systems which must then starve on the vine. The resulting dilemma is well stated by Herschel Kanter:

> Thus, if things continue as they have, we will have a Navy that cannot do what it is most clearly designed for: attack the Soviet Union or possibly other "high threat" areas. But because it is designed as it is, it is poorly suited to do what we would like, namely control the seas in wartime against attacks from Backfire bombers and cruise missile submarines while providing peacetime and crisis presence over the oceans.[58]

A fundamental question must be raised: what indeed is the worst case situation? To be sure, the possibility of outright war with the USSR captures, indeeds rivets, attention. Assuredly a viable strategy must be devised to cope with such a contingency, however unlikely it may be. But every day pressure mounts upon the sources of the natural resources which the economies of the United States and its allies find indispensable. In the long run, the position of the United States can be as effectively destroyed by slow but inexorable attrition in the Third World as by the dramatic confrontation of war.

1. "Reagan's Proposed Five-Year Navy Shipbuilding Program," Armed Forces Journal International, March 1982, p. 51.

2. Ibid.

3. Deborah M. Kyle, "Navy's 34% of FY83 Defense Budget Sustains Hefty Ship/Aircraft Buy," Armed Forces Journal International, March 1982, p. 58.

4. W. Eric Casey, "Top Ten Weapons Programs Swallow 13% of Total DOD FY83 Budget," Armed Forces Journal International, March 1982, p. 52.

5. Clarence A. Robinson, Jr., "Aircraft Modifications to Stretch Over Next Five Years," Aviation Week & Space Technology, 21 September 1981, p. 48.

6. David M. North, "Emphasis in Navy Budget Shifts Toward Expansion," Aviation Week & Space Technology, 15 February 1982, p. 22.

7. Clarence A. Robinson, Jr., "Maritime Superiority Goal Keyed to 600-Ship Fleet," Aviation Week & Space Technology, 31 August 1981, p. 39.

8. "Navy Stressing Survival of Fleet in Nuclear War," Aviation Week & Space Technology, 8 March 1982, pp. 50-51.

9. Howard W. Serig, Jr., "The Iowa Class: Needed Once Again," in Paul Stillwell, ed., Naval Review 1982 (Annapolis, Maryland: U.S. Naval Institute, 1982), p. 143.

10. "Reagan's Proposed Five Year Navy Shipbuilding Program."

11. "Navy Secretary Urges Building Balanced Offensive Capability," Aviation Week & Space Technology, 31 August 1981, p. 45.

12. Labayle Couhat, p. 722.

13. Mitchell, p. 7.

14. Ibid., p. 9.

15. Ibid.

16. MccGwire, Six Hundred Ships: The Navy and National Security, Part II: The Cost.

17. Ibid.

18. Robert W. Komer, "Maritime Strategy Vs. Coalition Defense," Foreign Affairs, Summer 1982, p. 1133.

19. Mitchell, p. 11.

20. Charles D. Allen, Jr., The Uses of Navies in Peacetime (Washington, D.C.: American Enterprise Institute for Public Policy Research, 1980), pp. 4-5.

21. Norman Friedman, Carrier Air Power (New York, New York: The Rutledge Press, 1981), p. 152.

22. Allen, Jr., p. 22.

23. Friedman.

24. Labayle Couhat, p. 705.

25. Ibid.

26. Alan H. Shaw, Costs of Expanding and Modernizing the Navy's Carrier-Based Air Forces (Washington, D.C.: Congressional Budget Office, May 1982), p. 4.

27. Richard Halloran, "Pentagon Chooses Grumman F-14 Jet As Navy's Fighter," The New York Times, 2 August 1982, pp. 1, 11.

28. Robinson, Jr., "Maritime Superiority Goal Keyed to 600-Ship Fleet," p. 47.

29. Ibid.

30. Robinson, Jr., "Backfire Threat Spurs F-14 Upgrading."

31. Gunston, p. 194.

32. Robert R. Ropelewski, "F-14 Performance Up With F101 Engines," Aviation Week & Space Technology, 19 October 1982, p. 44.

33. Walter Maguire, "The Phoenix Factor," Air Combat, March 1979, p. 62.

34. Ibid.

35. Robert R. Ropelewski, "October Delivery Slated for AIM-54Cs," Aviation Week & Space Technology, 21 September 1981, p. 81.

36. Ibid., p. 83.

37. Art Hanley, "Sharpening the Claws of the Tomcat," Proceedings: United States Naval Institute, June 1982, p. 110.

38. Robinson, Jr., "Backfire Threat Spurs F-14 Upgrading," pp. 50-51.

39. Ropelewski, "F-14 Performance Up With F101 Engines," pp. 44-45.

40. Ibid., p. 44.

41. Shaw, p. 43.

42. "Improvements in Works On A-6E, EA-6B Aircraft," Aviation Week & Space Technology, 21 September 1981, p. 88.

43. Ibid., pp. 88-90.

44. Shaw, pp. 17-18.

45. Ibid.

46. Benjamin F. Schemmer, "Navy Tells SecDef Budge Crunch Will Require Slowing F-18 Buys by 40-50%," Armed Forces Journal International, July 1980, p. 21.

47. "Navy, Manufacturer Concur On Fiscal 1982 F-18 Price," Aviation Week & Space Technology, 11 October 1982, p. 29.

48. Ibid.

49. Ibid.

50. Perrin Clausen, "Test Unit Opposes F/A-18 Attack Role," Aviation Week & Space Technology, 8 November 1982, p. 26.

51. John A. Williams, "U.S. Navy Missions and Force Structure: A Critical Reappraisal," Armed Forces And Society, Summer 1981, pp. 522-523.

52. Francis J. West. "NATO II: Common Boundaries for Common Interests," Naval War College Review, volume 34, January-February 1981, p. 65.

53. Hearings before the U.S. House of Representatives Committee on Armed Services on the Department of Defense Authorization for Appropriations for Fiscal Year 1980, 95th Congress (Washington, D.C.:

U.S. Government Printing Office, 1979), p. 841.

54. Admiral Stansfield Turner, USN (ret.), and Captain George Thibault, USN, "Preparing For The Unexpected: The Need For A New Military Strategy," Foreign Affairs, Fall 1982, pp. 126-127.

55. Admiral Elmo R. Zumwalt, Jr., USN (ret.), "Naval Battles We Could Lose", International Security Review, Summer 1982, p. 146.

56. Anthony H. Cordesman, "Power Projection and the War at Sea," Armed Forces International, September 1982, p. 44.

57. "Are Big Warships Doomed?" Newsweek, 17 May 1982, p. 45.

58. Herschel Kanter, "The Fleet for the 21st Century," National Defense, February 1981, p. 40.

XII
Force Projection at Sea

What is to be done? It must be clearly understood that the death of U.S. and allied economies through slow strangulation in "peacetime" can be as much a worst case situation as any dramatic "decisive battle" in time of war. Moreoever, the USSR is not the only nor the most likely challenge the United States must confront in the world. The United States must be able to bring seaborne airpower and an effective amphibious capability to bear in the far reaches of the world. From the standpoint of both strategy and cost the United States cannot afford super carrier battle groups that are too few in number, too vulnerable to destruction, and demand too many expensive surface escorts. Funds poured into super carrier battle groups, moreover, are monies denied to new and more effective technological developments. Numbers are important. Not even the most awesome warship can be in more than one place at a time. War cannot be waged unscathed, losses in hard fighting are inevitable. The widespread proliferation of modern weaponry means that operations in virtually any corner of the globe will encounted sophisticated opposition and cannot be carried out with impunity.

What are the major factors that determine the size and cost of the U.S. Navy? A misguided wartime mission, frontal assault upon the USSR, can devour funds and reduce the fleet to an array of very costly warships, so limited in number as to be both vulnerable to decisive destruction and inadequate to defend the sealanes upon which the survival of the United States and its allies depend. To attempt to fight simultaneously in every ocean of the world would demand an immense fleet.

In peacetime, the tradition of forward deployments in the Mediterranean and Pacific fix the basic numbers in the carrier fleet and, through the escorts needed, the rest of the surface navy as well. In peace and war, the conviction that a two super carrier battle

125

group, employing conventional aircraft, is necessary to be effective also drives the fundamental composition of the fleet.

How can the U.S. Navy be reconfigured? In a war with the Soviet Union, attack upon the Russian homeland -- if it must come to that -- ought to be entrusted to missile firing submarines. Thus relieved of a suicidal burden, the United States fleet can be equipped with warships that are less highly sophisticated, less narrowly specialized, less costly, and more numerous.

Is it feasible to attempt to wage campaigns in every ocean on the face of the earth simultaneously? The essence of strategy is not to scatter forces widely but rather to concentrate forces at the times and places needed to win decisive results. To attempt to be strong everywhere will only ensue in U.S. forces being weak in every quarter and open to defeat in detail. Another strategic imperative is that military power must be dedicated to the most important tasks that clamor for attention, not parcelled out to all.

Forward deployment must be assessed anew. Continuous forward deployments have stretched the fleet dangerously thin, imposed unequal -- and unfair -- burdens on crews and their families, and wrought a maintenance and logistic nightmare. Customary deployments also present the Soviets with targets conveniently fixed in certain habitual geographic locations. Also, carriers are now needed in areas other than the traditional Mediterranean and Pacific. United States carrier airpower must be flexible to deploy freely to the Indian Ocean, the coasts of Africa, and the Caribbean.

The great majority of the super carrier fleet should be held in U.S. waters.[1] Thus homeported the carriers could be better maintained, crew morale could be improved, highly trained technical personnel retained, and the warships brought to a high state of readiness to respond to unpredictable exigencies.

This is not to deny U.S. naval presence in areas of vital interest to the United States. Indeed, a super carrier and medium carrier, on rotation, should be deployed in the Indian Ocean, the theatre farthest from the United States. Perhaps a homeport could be established in Australia for U.S. naval forces operating in the Indian Ocean. United States forces might be politically more welcome in Australia than elsewhere. Australia is a democratic nation, far more stable than many other countries in Southwest Asia.

Elsewhere, battle groups should be built around Tomahawk missile armed cruisers or heavy destroyers and attack submarines. Such groups should be rotated, at six month intervals, to the Northwest Pacific, the Mediterranean, and the Norwegian Sea.

The traditional two super carrier battle group can

be reconstituted as well. V/STOL aviation has made considerable advances in recent years. Many advantages are offered by V/STOL aircraft which can complement, rather than rival, conventional warplane operations.[2] V/STOL planes can fly and provide air cover when weather conditions or battle damage make conventional air operations impossible. Such V/STOL machines as the Marines' AV-8A or the Royal Navy Sea Harrier function independent of the deck cycles that govern conventional aircraft operations and can thus be launched between deck cycles to provide continuous air cover. Damage to catapults, arresting gear, or even flight deck will not halt V/STOL operations.

Two major exercises in particular have demonstrated the capabilities of the Harrier when deployed in close cooperation with a conventional super carrier. Over a three month period in the summer of 1981, 20 Marine Harriers were deployed on board the USS Nassau, a 40,000 ton Tarawa class LHA, in the Mediterranean.[3] An LHA so configured carried enough parts, equipment, and munitions to support the Harrier force for thirty days of intensive operations. Unhampered by deck cycles, Harriers were able to respond immediately whenever called upon for close air support in maneuvers and could maintain a continuous flow of supporting warplanes. In the STOL mode, Harriers were launched every ten seconds and were simulating attack on designated targets within five minutes of take off.[4] To augment carrier air defense, the AV-8As were armed with Sidewinder missiles and, under the overall direction of Gumman E-2Cs, flew air patrol for as long as three hours at a stretch.[5]

In August and September of 1981, five Sea Harriers and the light carrier Invincible of the Royal Navy operated with the U.S. super carrier Eisenhower from Norfolk, Virginia to Norway and Great Britain to Portugal.[6] Sea Harrier is specifically configured for the air defense role. It is equipped with Ferranti air to air radar and a sophisticated radar warning display. It is armed with four Sidewinder missiles and two 30mm. cannon. The Sea Harriers cooperated effectively with U.S. F-14s in the air defense mission. As Roy Braybrook notes:

> At one stage a combat air patrol was required against a stated threat axis and 801 Squadron provided Sea Harriers on station for 90 hours non-stop, a remarkable achievement for a five-aircraft, seven-pilot unit and one that drew praise from the U.S. Navy.[7]

These exercises clearly demonstrate that V/STOL warplanes based on a medium or light carrier can effectively augment and complement a super carrier equipped with conventional aircraft. Future carrier task forces might well comprise a super carrier, a 40,000 ton medium carrier, and, to furnish fire support for amphibious operations, one of the reactivated battleships.

These fundamental changes in Navy missions, practices, and operational structure call for a change in the composition of the fleet. The two nuclear fueled super carriers of the Improved Nimitz class that have been authorized should be cancelled before precious funding for them is appropriated. These funds could then be devoted to construction of carriers better suited to the sealane protection and amphibious missions.

Dedicated to defense of the super carrier in the role of frontal attack on the USSR, the Ticonderoga class of air defense cruiser should be substantially reduced. The Ticonderoga and her sister, the Yorktown, are scheduled to enter service in 1983 and 1984 respectively. Twenty eight ships of the Ticonderoga class are currently projected.[8] The Ticonderogas are quite expensive and will cost an estimated 1.02 billion Fiscal Year 1982 dollars each.[9]

Primary responsibility for air defense of the fleet must be entrusted to F-14 interceptors and other fighters. The Ticonderogas should be configured as missile cruisers, armed with the nuclear warhead version of Tomahawk.[10] The Ticonderogas should be deployed, as the central warships of cruise missile battle groups, to the crucial areas of the Northwest Pacific, the Eastern Mediterranean, and the Norwegian Sea. In this role, perhaps twelve Ticonderogas would be sufficient to assure regularly scheduled deployments.

The Navy's proposed new class of destroyer, the DDG-51, must also be carefully scrutinized. Like the Ticonderoga, the purpose of the DDG-51 is to defend the super carrier in its direct onslaught against the Soviet Union. Although designated a multipurpose destroyer, the DDG-51 is primarily an antiaircraft ship. Initial authorization for the first ship of the class is planned for Fiscal year 1985, and the Navy hopes to eventually secure 63 of the new destroyers.[11]

But the DDG-51 cannot carry the ammunition load of the Spruance class destroyer.[12] Although equipped with a helicopter landing platform, the DDG-51 does not have a hangar. Full load weight of the design stands at 8,500 tons, 2,000 tons more than the originally conceived maximum limit.[13] Projected cost is now pegged at slightly more than the Ticonderogas.[14] Hence the DDG-51 will be an expensive warship designed to support a suicidal mission.

But the U.S. Navy does need new heavy destroyers. Many of the destroyers now in service will be relegated to the scrapheap in the late 1980s and early 1990s.

What the fleet needs is a genuinely multipurpose and versatile warship. An improved Kidd class, based on the Spruance, could meet the needs of the Navy quite well. Very well armed, the Kidd is equipped with two Standard antiaircraft missile launchers, ASROC antisubmarine rockets, Harpoon surface to surface missiles, two Phalanx air defense machine cannon systems, two five inch cannon, and hangars for two helicopters.[15] The Kidd also features the welcome protection of Kevlar and of alloy armor. The new SM-2 version of the Standard missile can be readily employed by the Kidd. A towed sonar array can be added without difficulty. For the money to be invested in the Ticonderoga and DDG-51 classes, many more Kidd class warships could be purchased.

Yet the need for carrier airpower remains paramount. It is impossible to undertake operations without air cover and air support. Land air bases in the Third World are hostage to explosive political instabilities, knife edged regional rivalries, and tyrannical regimes.

Best suited to such operations would be the 40,000 ton short take off carrier proposed by Rear Admiral George Jessen of the U.S. Naval Air Systems Command in 1978. Powered by compact gas turbine engines and utilizing a large container ship hull, the carrier would be fast and capacious. It would be equipped with a ski-jump ramp to facilitate take off and arresting gear to assure short landing.[16] A low power catapult would be fitted to launch S-3A antisubmarine planes. Such a 40,000 ton STO carrier could be constructed at approximately one-third the cost of a Nimitz type super carrier.[17]

It must be emphasized that the STO carrier would employ conventional warplanes now in service and would not be restricted to V/STOL aircraft. The vitally important airborne early warning Grumman E-2C would be an integral part of the air group. A full strike and intercept combat control center would be readily accommodated in a 40,000 ton warship.

In the late summer and fall of 1982, it should be noted, the Navy completed extensive testing of the F-14 in ski-jump launches at the Naval Air Test Center. A nine degree ramp may reduce the take off distance for an F-14 to 800 feet.[18] Certainly General Electric engines could improve this performance considerably.

Four 40,000 ton STO carriers should be secured to augment U.S. air power at sea. Four such ships could be built for the price of one and one-third Improved Nimitz super carriers. It must be stressed that a STO carrier would not be a substitute for a super carrier. It could operate in conjunction with a super carrier in a two carrier task force. Or it could be the center, in wartime, of an antisubmarine task force dedicated to sealane patrol and protection.

The 40,000 ton carrier would be especially valuable in support of amphibious operations, providing air cover and close air support. A Marine Corps aviation air group for such a mission might be made up of twelve F-18 fighters and 24 AV-8 fighter bombers. In such a situation, the 40,000 ton carrier would be part of a task force including a super carrier, providing air defense over a wide area, and very likely a rejuvenated battleship furnishing heavy gunfire and Tomahawk missile support. A number of internal Navy studies have highlighted the desirability of 40,000 ton carriers in the amphibious assault role.

What can be said of the current state of V/STOL aviation? During the past six years many studies, including Quo Vadis and the Air Master Plan, have underlined the value of V/STOL aircraft to air power at sea.[19] Flexibility in basing, ease of dispersion for survivability, swift response, and high rate of use are all cited as key advantages of V/STOL warplanes.

The performance of the British Sea Harrier in the Falkland Islands War vindicated V/STOL warplanes in the crucible of conflict -- the ultimate test. It must be emphasized that, although the Sea Harrier is configured and equipped for air combat, its main role is defense of the fleet against long range bombers. Airborne early warning in the North Atlantic would be provided by Nimrod patrol planes flying from bases in Great Britain. In the South Atlantic conflict the Harriers were confronted with fighters and fighter bombers. The Harriers also fought at a singular disadvantage -- bereft of airborne early warning. The Harriers had to contend against numerical odds, 28 Sea Harriers were pitted against some 120 warplanes. In air to air combat, Sea Harriers shot down 32 confirmed Argentine planes with no loss of their own.[20] Two Sea Harriers were lost to antiaircraft fire and four were destroyed by accidents.

Serviceability and reliability of the V/STOL fighter proved to be superb. At daybreak, 95 percent of the Harriers were ready to fly and, after averaging six sorties each day, more than 80 percent of the fighters remained capable of combat by nightfall.[21] Harriers flew and fought in appalling winter weather: poor visibility, gale winds, and seas so storm tossed that only the ski-jumps pitched the fighters high enough to clear the waves.

An assessment of the V/STOL fighter's performance must take into account the factors that seriously handicapped the Argentine Air Force. Argentine warplanes were compelled to fly to the end of their maximum radius. British antiaircraft missile defenses forced the Argentines to attack at very low level, vulnerable to Sea Harriers and point defense weapons.

Upon reaching the target areas, Argentine planes lacked enough fuel to engage in dogfighting maneuvers or use afterburner for acceleration. Ghastly weather impartially hampered both sides.

At this stage in its development the V/STOL fighter should not be considered a viable substitute for the conventional warplane in the air superiority role. As large scale exercises have repeatedly proven, the characteristics of the Harrier make it an ideal complement to the conventional interceptor, providing continuous close air cover. But F-14, F-15, and F-16 must continue to be the front line of U.S. fighter defense.

A much improved version of the Harrier will come into service with the Royal Air Force and the U.S. Marine Corps in the course of the 1980s. As many as 354 of the new AV-8Bs may become operational with Marine aviation.[22] In the close support mission, given a 1,000 foot short take off run, the AV-8B can carry twelve 570 lb. bombs to a target area 161 nautical miles distant and remain on call over that area for one hour.[23] In the interdiction role, the AV-8B can unleash seven 570 lb. bombs against a target 629 nautical miles away.[24] A 25mm. machine cannon will be an integral part of the AV-8B's armament. A wide variety of weapons can be employed by the new Harrier, such as the Rockeye cluster bomb and the devastating anti-tank Maverick missile. Accuracy is aided immensely by an angle rate bombing system incorporating laser and television trackers and a weapon delivery computer.

Many significant improvements are embodied in the AV-8B. It is estimated that detailed changes in the engine will slash maintenance manpower requirements in half and cut the engine failure rate by 35 percent.[25] McDonnell Douglas has employed the cockpit design experience gained from the F-15 to good effect in the new Harrier. Much better all around visibility is afforded by the raised cockpit, and a head up display and installation of many controls on the stick and throttle are valuable new features.

Much safer, and easier, handling in the critical stage of transition from vertical to horizontal flight is assured by a number of design features and new equipment.[26] A change in the reaction control nozzle and wider wingspan help to control the roll rate more effectively. Airlift is secured at lower airspeeds by a larger wing and new single slotted flaps. Above all, a three axis stability augmentation system makes transitional maneuvers far less demanding and hazardous.

In the fighter role, the AV-8B will be armed with four of the new all aspect model of the Sidewinder missile, proven remarkably effective in the Falkland

Islands and Lebanon Wars. Swift acceleration is the strongest card the Harrier has to play. Thrust can also be vectored in flight to confront an opponent with sudden and unpredictable maneuvers. Roy Braybrook outlines another key point:

> A further important factor is that the Sea Harrier pilot knows that his aircraft will not "depart" with the jets aft. If he should get into difficulty with the jets down, he can always select zero nozzle angle and the aircraft will recover immediately. Even junior pilots therefore manoeuvre the Sea Harrier with complete confidence, knowing that they will not lose control of the aircraft, and they can thus take on fighters which in theory have much better turning performance.[27]
> (emphasis mine)

Air to air maneuvers have shown that Sea Harriers, in defensive combat, can hold their own even against the formidable F-15s and F-16s.[28]

Installation of the Hughes APG-65 dual mode radar would greatly enhance the AV-8B's air combat capability. Designed for the F/A-18, the Hughes radar has proven remarkable reliable and trouble free. Less versatile, but lighter in weight and less costly are the Emerson APQ-159 and the General Electric G-200. With such radar it would be possible to arm the AV-8B with Sparrow missiles and the "fire and forget" AMRAAM now in development.

In the event of war with the USSR, the United States must defend the vital sealanes with every resource it can muster. This will be no easy task. The armada of Russian submarines grows swiftly more numerous and effective. The proportion of the Soviet undersea fleet deployed at any given time has substantially increased in recent years. Hence the Soviet submarine threat cannot be thwarted by attacking bases in the USSR.

Moreover the modern freighter or tanker is a giant ship. Even a relatively small number of such ships sunk would be a very heavy blow. The impact of severe shipping losses upon U.S. and allied fortunes in the East Asian, Southwest Asian and Western European theatres could be swift and catastrophic -- even in a conflict of relatively short duration.

United States' and allied antisubmarine frigates will surely be hard pressed in such a war. Clearly, the antisubmarine forces of the United States and its allies must be augmented. Fortunately, an effective means is at hand to reinforce the crucial campaign against the submarine. James J. Mulquin outlines the project now being successfully tested:

The baseline ARAPAHO system involves the development of an aviation facility in modular form, with major components configured to resemble standard metal freight containers. Major components -- the hangar, flight deck, accommodations array and fuel farm -- are designed to be handled by commercial gantry cranes and standard pier equipment. . . .

Estimates are that the entire facility, weighing 1,200 tons, can be loaded in 10 to 14 hours and made ready for aircraft recovery within 20 hours. Units are self-sustaining -- heated, powered, lighted and vented -- and on arrival at pierside already contain the aviation shops, maintenance gear, spare parts and support needed of an aviation detachment at sea.

Virtually any Navy or Marine Corps helicopter is compatible: the UH-1, SH-2F, CH-46, CH/RH-53 and the SH-60.[29]

Such installations would not be limited to ASW but could serve other purposes: airborne mine countermeasures, amphibious assault, defense against antiship missiles, and many others. As many as four to six helicopters could be operated. Naval Reserves would be especially well suited to man these aviation units.[30]

ARAPAHO is a concept whose time has indeed come. Many modern cargo ships are very large, even 50,000 tons, and quite fast, as swift as 33 knots. They are virtually ready made helo or V/STOL aircraft carriers. So, once more in history, the armed merchantman comes into its own.

The wartime purposes and peacetime practices of the United States Navy must be fundamentally reformulated and shaped anew. Only thus can the security of the sealanes, upon which the fate of the United States and its key partners depends, be assured in time of war. So reshaped, the U.S. fleet could cope effectively with other conflicts in areas of the world of vital interest to the United States and its allies.

134

1. Cf. Captain William K. Sullivan, USN, "Now is the Time to: Rethink, Redesign, and Redeploy Naval Aviation," Naval War College Review, volume 35, March-April 1982, pp. 11-12.

2. "Development AV-8B to Fly in October." Aviation Week & Space Technology, 21 September 1981, p. 63.

3. "Marine Harrier Use Wins Interest of Parent Service," Aviation Week & Space Technology, 21 September 1981, p. 64.

4. Ibid., pp. 64, 67.

5. Ibid., p. 67.

6. Roy Braybrook, "Sea Harrier Fully Operational," International Defense Review, January 1982, p. 49.

7. Ibid.

8. Labayle Couhat, p. 737.

9. Peter. T. Tarpgaard, Naval Surface Combatants in the 1990s: Prospects and Possibilities (Washington, D.C.: Congressional Budget Office, April 1981), p. 38.

10. Ibid., pp. 20-21.

11. Norman Polmar, "The U.S. Navy: A New Destroyer Class," Proceedings, U.S. Naval Institute, August 1982, p. 122.

12. Ibid., p. 123.

13. Ibid.

14. Ibid., p. 124.

15. Labayle Couhat, pp. 742, 744.

16. Norman Friedman, Carrier Air Power (New York, New York: The Rutledge Press, 1981), pp. 157-159.

17. Ibid., p. 159.

18. "Navy Testing F-14 in Ski-Jump Launches," Aviation Week & Space Technology, 6 September 1982. p. 43.

19. "Development AV-8B to Fly in October."

20. "British Harriers Averaged Six Sorties Per Day," Aviation Week & Space Technology.

21. Derek Wood and Mark Hewish, "The Falklands Conflict: Part 1: the air war," International Defense Review, August 1982, p. 980.

22. Roy Braybrook, "AV-8B Harrier II," Air International, February 1982, p. 102.

23. Clarence A. Robinson, Jr., "Industry Proposes Supersonic V/STOL Development," Aviation Week & Space Technology, 12 January 1981, p. 36.

24. Ibid.

25. Braybrook, "AV-8B Harrier II," p. 67.

26. "AV-8B 'easier to fly than Harriers'," Flight International, 16 October 1982, p. 1093.

27. Braybrook, "Sea Harrier Fully Operational", p. 50.

28. Ibid.

29. Jim Mulquin, "ARAPAHO Update," Naval Aviation News, April 1982, pp. 21-22.

30. James J. Mulquin, "The Navy ARAPAHO Project -- A Status Report," Naval Reserve Association News, February 1982, p. 6.

XIII
Conclusion

The fundamental purposes the U.S. Navy should serve are the maritime interests of the United States. Increasingly the United States is a maritime nation, ineluctably entwined in a world economy whose links are seaborne. The United States is the source upon which much of the world relies for such vital elements as food, coal, and wood products. A flow of imported oil and key minerals is needed to supply a flourishing U.S. economy. The manufacture of globally integrated industrial products is another fundamental feature of the world economy.

The main function of the United States Navy, in cooperation with the fleets of allied nations, must be to secure untrammeled use of the global sealanes in peace and war. The U.S. fleet must be capable of bringing appropriate means to bear to influence events in regions of vital interest to the United States. A viable U.S. economy and polity rests upon the achievement of these objectives.

What measures are needed to guard the sealanes and assure an effective U.S. presence in distant areas of the world? A unified strategy must ensure the close cooperation of land, sea, and tactical air forces. No one branch of the armed forces should assume a dominant role, all have their distinctive parts to play. The strengths of the different services can complement each other. The aircraft carrier can go where land bases cannot be found and land based warplanes may operate where the carrier dare not risk its presence. In United States strategy, the Navy is indispensable. But, by itself, the U.S. Navy cannot be the arm of decision in a struggle with a Eurasian super power.

The most serious military shortcoming is the dearth of sufficient air and sea transport needed to deploy and supply troops in major theatres around the globe. To be sure, an additional 50 C-5Bs and 44 KC-10As will substantially augment U.S. airlift capability. Even so, airlift will fall short seven million ton miles/day

below   the   requirement   established   by   the
Congressionally Mandated Mobility Study.[1] Confronted
by simultaneous crises in Europe and the Persian Gulf,
airlift of bulky and odd shaped cargo could fall 66
percent below requirements.[2]

Another problem complicates the airlift picture.
Troops and cargo flown by strategic transports to a
theatre must then transfer to tactical transports to
deploy into combat zones.   A legendary workhorse, the
Lockheed C-130 tactical transport is aging and worn.
It will be necessary to replace the C-130 fleet in the
late 1980s.

The McDonnell Douglas C-17 was designed to surmount
these problems.   Loading troops and weapons at military
bases in the United States, the C-17 would fly them
directly to relatively short, rough airfields in the
conflict arenas, eliminating the need for transfer and
the tactical transport fleet.[3]

Outsize cargo transports are needed as soon as
possible, and the C-5Bs are the only aircraft readily
available to meet the need.   But the Lockheed C-5 can
never be a substitute for the C-17.   The Air Force
program for 144 C-17s should be strongly supported.

The deplorable state of United States sealift,
merchant shipping, and shipbuilding capabilities should
arouse serious concern on the part of all Americans.
The U.S. merchant fleet has suffered severely from
neglect -- and this in an era when the very lifeblood
of the U.S. economy flows along oceanborne arteries.
Such neglect now levies a heavy penalty upon U.S.
sealift capabilities.   The condition of the U.S.
shipbuilding industry will make such deficiencies
difficult to remedy.   United States shipyards suffer
from the afflictions that beset other basic U.S.
industries.   Plants are obsolete, inefficient, and
labor intensive.   New machinery, such as automatic
welders and digitally controlled fabrication tools, are
desperately needed.   Skilled workers, such as mold and
pattern makers, steam fitters, electricians, and
systems engineers, are in very short supply.
Procurement bottlenecks are to be found in a wide array
of vital components, such as thrust bearings, over size
castings, and parts made from exotic alloys.

United States sealift and shipbuilding needs can be
addressed by nothing less than a comprehensive national
maritime policy, dedicated to rejuvenation of the
United States Merchant Marine and extensive
modernization of U.S. shipyards and propulsion
machinery factories.   Only a revived merchant fleet can
provide enough trained Americans to crew ships pressed
into service in time of emergency or war.   New long
term mobilization plans, systematic and thoroughgoing,
must be worked out.   Only thus can new merchant ships
be appropriately designed and constructed.   Features of

significance for wartime operations, such as helicopter
facilities, could thus be installed.

A factor complicating the sealift situation is that
the container ship, the workhorse of current merchant
shipping, is ill suited to handle military cargo. Best
configured for military use is the "roll on, roll off"
cargo ship. The Congressionally Mandated Mobility
Study underlines a paucity of Ro-Ro ships needed to
meet the demands of military sealift. To be sure the
Military Sealift Command will secure four of the
extremely useful Maine class ships. It is intended to
convert eight Sea-Land container ships to the Ro-Ro
configuration. Even so, it may be wise to revive the
Security class program. This plan envisaged the
construction of 14 new cargo ships for the MSC.
Weighing 48,860 tons at full load, the Security class
ship would feature a helicopter pad and stern vehicle
cargo ramp.[4]

The hypnotic fascination of current U.S. naval
leadership with horizontal escalation and a headlong
super carrier assault on the Soviet homeland must be
broken. The U.S. fleet may not be able, on its own, to
win a struggle with the USSR, but the U.S. Navy,
through suicidal folly, assuredly could lose such a
war. The legacy of maritime history and the
imperatives of geography command the navy to take up
the crucial roles of guardian of the sealanes and
protector of the national interest.

If the U.S. Navy is to be capable of bringing
effective influence to bear in the far reaches of the
world, amphibious warfare units must be assigned a much
higher priority. Block obsolescence now looms ahead
for many amphibious ships of the U.S. fleet. Indeed,
during the decade of the 1990s, the U.S. Navy will lose
all but six of its present fleet of 61 amphibious
ships.

Three amphibious ships must be constructed each
year over the next twenty years just to maintain the
current level of capability.[5] Air cushion vehicles are
central to a much more effective amphibious assault
strategy. Launched far from shore and cruising at high
speed, air cushion vehicles can sharply reduce the
vulnerability of amphibious shipping. Even more
significant, ACVs can land troops on more than 70
percent of the shores of the world. The planned
acquisition of air cushion vehicles, the LCAC program,
is a justifiably high priority for the Marine Corps.

Airpower at sea is absolutely essential. In many
areas land bases for tactical air are not readily
available. In some cases land air bases are at the
mercy of unstable political conditions. What kind of
carrier airpower is needed to protect the sealanes
and support amphibious operations?

The two planned Improved Nimitz class super

carriers and their associated surface escorts, designed
for direct attack against the Russian Heartland, should
be cancelled. Instead four 40,000 ton medium carriers
should be secured. Such a medium carrier would be
equipped with a ski-jump ramp, arresting gear, and a
low energy catapult. Medium carriers could serve three
major purposes: to augment air defense in a carrier
battle group, as the central ship in an antisubmarine
task force, or to provide close air support to an
amphibious operation. Configured for the amphibious
support role, a medium carrier would embark twelve
Marine F-18 fighters and 24 Marine AV-8B V/STOL fighter
bombers. Medium carriers would thus complement the
super carrier in the vital roles of air defense and
amphibious operations. They could play a valuable part
in defense of the sealanes against the large, and
increasingly more lethal, Soviet submarine fleet. It
is estimated that a medium 40,000 ton carrier would
cost but one-third the price of a Nimitz super
carrier.[6] A versatile warship, the medium carrier
would enable the U.S. Navy to deploy airpower in more
areas at sea.

Of critical importance to U.S. carrier airpower is
the Grumman F-14 long range interceptor. Only the F-14
can defend the fleet against the Soviet Backfire attack
warplane. Only the long reach of the F-14 can counter
the arsenal of sophisticated weapons in the inventories
of so many nations around the world. Such modern
weaponry places an increasing premium upon long
operating range for carrier based warplanes.

Re-engining the F-14 with the General Electric F101
DFE engines should proceed as swiftly as possible.
Already tested, the GE engines virtually eliminate
engine stall, a matter of particular importance during
launch. Throttles can be rapidly manipulated at all
angles of attack and speeds. Engine response is swift,
precise, and smooth, consequently increasing
acceleration rates. Moreover combat range is
considerably extended.[7]

Serious consideration should be given to the
development of an attack version of the F-14. A large
aircraft, the F-14 could accommodate the electronic
systems needed for the strike role and can carry a
substantial payload. Certainly the F-14 is quite
capable of defending itself.

The development of V/STOL aviation for the fleet
should be emphasized. The V/STOL aircraft should not
be viewed as a substitute for the conventional
warplane, they should be seen as complementary to each
other. During the past six years studies such as the
Air Master Plan and Quo Vadis have underlined the value
of V/STOL airplanes to airpower at sea.[8] Moreover, the
value of V/STOL aviation has been borne out in practice
in numerous exercises, most notably the deployment of

20 Marine AV-8As onboard the LHA Nassau with the Mediterranean fleet during the summer of 1982.[9]

Independent of deck cycles, V/STOL aircraft can provide continuous close air cover and constantly available close support to ground forces. V/STOL planes can fly in weather that would prevent conventional aircraft carrier operations. V/STOL aircraft can fly from helicopter pads on destroyers and frigates. In the Falkland Islands War, British Sea Harriers extended their combat patrol time by refueling from destroyers.

The AV-8B, now in the process of development, embodies many detailed changes which greatly improve stability in take off and landing, engine reliability, safety, and maintenance.[10] A multi-mode radar should be installed, thus fitting the new Harrier for a more effective air to air as well as air to ground role. So equipped, the AV-8B could employ the new AMRAAM, "fire and forget," active radar homing air to air missile.

Command and control of U.S. forces configured for the rapid deployment role remains a crucial issue. The U.S. Rapid Deployment Joint Task Force has been supplanted by the U.S. Central Command which is entrusted with responsibility for the Indian Ocean, Persian Gulf, and Southwest Asian areas. A potentially hazardous division of these areas between the U.S. European and Pacific Commands has thus been alleviated.

However preoccupation with the problems posed by Southwest Asia should not divert attention from other critical areas. such as the South Atlantic and Southern Africa. U.S. rapid deployment forces must think and plan in global terms. Major crises often erupt in unexpected places.

It will be essential to maintain a multi-service headquarters. Joint operations are among the most challenging aspects of the military art. Necessarily complex, such cooperative military ventures demand long experience in planning and working together by all branches of the armed services. Improvisation, in joint operations, is an invitation to disaster.

A coalition strategy must be an essential feature of U.S. policy. Such a coalition strategy is the logical strategic corollary to the position of the United States in the world economy. It reflects as well the fundamental political values and human concerns that the United States and its key partners share.

British bases, especially Diego Suarez, are indispensable to the western position in the Indian Ocean. Quiet British influence plays a significant part in Oman, strategic keystone of the Persian Gulf. The Falkland Islands War clearly proved that the British armed forces could carry out a major military operation 8,000 miles from the homeland, a campaign

142

crowned by success. Highly professional, well trained
and well led, Royal Marines and British Army units are
in the front rank of light infantry in the world today.
The Royal Navy will now keep in service three light
V/STOL carriers, two amphibious assault ships, and a
light command cruiser.

Moreover, the British now intend to expand their
formation earmarked for operations outside the European
area, the Fifth Brigade, into a full airborne unit. An
artillery regiment, an armored reconnaissance regiment,
and a helicopter squadron will be integrated into the
airborne brigade on a permanent basis.

France occupies a position of major strategic
importance in Northern and Central Africa and the
Indian Ocean. At the invitation of the African
governments concerned, French troops are stationed in
no less than five African nations. French forces
specifically organized, equipped, and trained for rapid
deployment missions include an airborne division, an
overseas infantry division, and units of the
redoubtable Foreign Legion. These units have been
called into action no less than eleven times since
1976, mounting operations in six African countries.
France maintains a balanced and versatile fleet
including two conventional aircraft carriers, a command
cruiser, and a helicopter carrier.

Although modest in size, Australian and New Zealand
forces occupy an important position in Southeast Asia.
In accord with the governments concerned, troops from
New Zealand are stationed in Singapore and squadrons of
Australian fighters are based in Malaysia. Australian
warships are committed to the Indian Ocean in support
of the U.S. fleet in those waters.

On order from Britain are Leander class frigates
and Scorpion light tanks for New Zealand forces. The
Australian Navy includes three guided missile
destroyers, three new guided missile frigates, six ASW
frigates, and 20 P-3 ASW patrol planes.[11] The
Australians plan to secure four more guided missile
frigates. Australian P-3 aircraft will be armed with
the Harpoon missile.

Responding to the surge of Soviet military strength
in the Far East and Indochina, Japan has embarked upon
a searching re-examination of its defense position and
military role. The geo-strategic position of Japan in
the Far East is indeed central. Japan blocks the
narrow straits through which the Soviet fleet must
debouch into Pacific waters. Without a neutral Japan
at her flank, Communist China would be ringed about by
foes. Without Japan as an ally, the United States
would be hard pressed to maintain a military position
in the Far East.

Although Japanese ground forces are quite modest,
Japan's air arm is respectable, and her fleet, as

befits a maritime nation, is not inconsiderable. Phantom fighters constitute the first line of air defense. The Japanese Maritime Self-Defense Force includes 33 destroyers, 16 frigates, 14 submarines, and 68 antisubmarine patrol planes.[12] Four of the destroyers are large, well armed ships each carrying three Sea King ASW helicopters. On order are eight new destroyers, two frigates, and three submarines.

A new five year defense program was approved in the summer of 1982 by the National Defense Council of Japan. During the years 1983 to 1987 the Ground Self-Defense Force would hope to acquire 373 battle tanks, 354 cannon, and 57 attack helos.[13] The air arm will be strengthened with 155 F-15 fighters, 101 close support attack planes, and nine E-2C airborne early warning and control aircraft.[14] Eleven destroyers, three frigates, and 75 P-3C Orion long range ASW patrol planes will join the Japanese fleet.[15]

Whether these goals will be achieved remains to be seen. The impact of world recession may undercut the program. However, even partial realization of these objectives would improve Japan's defensive position considerably. The new Prime Minister of Japan, Yasuhiro Nakasone, is well known as a proponent of increased defensive capabilities for Japan. But Nakasone has also promised to slash Japan's national budget deficits, a difficult task to reconcile with increased defense spending.

In the long run, Japan must take up an increasing share of responsibility for the air and naval defense of her territory and the sealanes upon which her economy is so utterly dependent. From the technological and industrial standpoints Japan is well suited to assume this burden. Thus can U.S. naval resources be concentrated in the troubled waters of Southwest Asia.

Can the United States and its allies cope with the challenge of the USSR and its partners in the Third World? It must be emphasized that Soviet intervention in the developing countries has been undertaken with great caution and deliberation. The Soviet Union and its partners have seized upon opportune situations in the Third World, moving to intervene where circumstances have been favorable and prospects of success appeared to be high. Nor have Soviet moves been made in situations where U.S. opposition might be anticipated.

Under these circumstances U.S. forces need not be massive in numbers to deter Soviet adventures in the Third World. United States' forces must be highly professional and appropriately organized and equipped for rapid deployment missions. So configured, U.S. and allied conventional forces can significantly influence the behavior of the USSR in the developing world.

However, as the Falkland Islands War and the Lebanon War of 1982 have clearly shown, challenges other than Soviet are far more likely to confront the United States and its allies. Bitter rivalries and internecine conflicts abound in critical areas of the world. Virtually all nations have now accummulated lethal arsenals of sophisticated weapons and built up substantial armed forces. During the period from 1972 to 1981 the developing nations purchased 6,630 fighters, 35,735 anti-aircraft missiles, 31,840 armored vehicles, and 54,555 pieces of artillery.[16] Effective operations, even in the farthest reaches of the globe, demand highly professional forces armed with the best of modern weapons.

Such events as the assassination of Sadat, the seizure of the Grand Mosque, and the plot against the government of Bahrain underline the internal vulnerability of many key regimes. Moreover, the frequent coups in vital mineral producing African countries highlight the violent instability afflicting many governments. Such recurrent internal difficulties emphasize the value of forces skilled in low intensity operations.

But the United States must not be locked into sustaining unpopular dictatorships in power, pro-American though some such regimes may be. Moreover such domestically unpopular governments are frequently highly vulnerable to pro-Soviet political movements. Rather the United States should help countries of the Third World to become genuinely independent and free from domination by either super power. Change is inevitable and should be welcomed. The United States should help support a framework within which peaceful change can be assured. Gradual change can ensure that the fruits of progress are not lost in the chaos of revolution and reaction. To help assure peaceful and effective change in the Third World will be the supreme challenge to United States' statecraft -- and navies are flexible and subtle instruments of diplomacy.

145

1. Schemmer, Budget Cutters Are Only Ones Likely to Win Battle Over C-5B/747F/C-17 Airlift Alternatives," p. 48.

2. Robinson, Jr., "USAF Seeks Continued Effort on C-17," p. 24.

3. Everett A. Chambers, "Airlift: Finding the Plane to Fit the Mission," Armed Forces Journal International, November 1982, p. 48.

4. Labayle Couhat, p. 803.

5. Miller, USA, "LCACs and the Lift Dilemma," p. 48.

6. Friedman, p. 159.

7. Ropelewski, "F-14 Performance Up With F101 Engines," pp. 44-45.

8. "Development AV-8B to Fly in October," p. 63.

9. "Marine Harrier Use Wins Interest of Parent Service," p. 64.

10. Braybrook, "AV-8B Harrier II," pp. 65,67.

11. Labayle Couhat, pp. 17-20.

12. The International Institute for Strategic Studies, The Military Balance 1982-1983, p. 87.

13. "Japanese Defense Council Approves Five-Year Plan," p. 99.

14. Ibid., p. 96.

15. Ibid.

16. Anthony H. Cordesman, "The Falklands: the Air War and Missile Conflict," Armed Forces Journal International, September 1982, p. 34.

Selected Bibliography

Documents

Cracknell, Captain William H., ed. <u>Understanding Soviet Naval Developments</u>. Washington, D.C.: Office of the Chief of Naval Operations, Department of the Navy, January 1981.

Headquarters, Rapid Deployment Joint Task Force, Public Affairs Office. <u>Fact Sheet</u>. MacDill AFB, Florida, June 1982.

Mitchell, Douglas D. <u>Shipbuilding Costs For General Purpose Forces In A 600-Ship Navy</u>. Washington, D.C.: Congressional Research Service, Library of Congress, February 16, 1982.

Shaw, Alan H. <u>Costs of Expanding and Modernizing the Navy's Carrier-Based Air Forces</u>. Washington, D.C.: Congressional Budget Office, May 1982.

Tarpgaard, Peter T. <u>Building a 600-Ship Navy: Costs, Timing, and Alternative Approaches</u>. Washington, D.C.: Congressional Budget Office, March 1982.

_____. <u>Naval Surface Combatants in the 1990s: Prospects and Possibilities</u>. Washington, D.C.: Congressional Budget Office, April 1981.

United Nations. <u>Yearbook of International Trade Statistics</u>, volume II. New York, New York: The United Nations, 1981.

United States Air Force. <u>Air Force Manual 1-1, Functions and Basic Doctrine of the United States Air Force</u>. Washington, D.C.: Headquarters USAF/XOX, February 1979.

U.S. Army Armor Center. <u>Organization and Equipment of the Soviet Army</u>. Fort Knox, Kentucky: U.S. Army Armor Center, 1981.

U.S. Department of Defense. <u>Soviet Military Power</u>. Washington, D.C.: U.S. Government Printing Office, [September, 1981].

148

Zakheim, Dov S. The Marine Corps in the 1980's: Prestocking Proposals, the Rapid Deployment Force, and Other Issues. Washington, D.C.: Congressional Budget Office, May 1980.

Books

Allen, Charles D. Jr. The Uses of Navies in Peacetime. Washington, D.C.: American Enterprise Institute for Public Policy Research, 1980.

Collins, John M. U.S.-Soviet Military Balance: Concepts and Capabilities, 1960-1980. New York, New York: McGraw-Hill Publications Co., 1980.

Council on Economics and National Security. Strategic Minerals: A Resource Crisis. New York, New York: National Strategy Information Center, 1981.

Deese, David A. and Nye, Joseph S., editors. Energy And Security. Cambridge, Massachusetts: Ballinger Publishing Company, 1981.

Dismukes, Bradford and McConnell, James M., editors. Soviet Naval Diplomacy. New York, New York: Pergamon Press, 1979.

Durch, William J. The Cuban Military In Africa And The Middle East: From Algeria to Angola. Alexandria, Virginia: Center For Naval Analyses, September 1977.

Friedman, Norman. Carrier Air Power. New York, New York: The Rutledge Press, 1981.

Gann, L.H. and Duignan, Peter. Africa South of the Sahara: The Challenge to Western Security. Stanford, California: Hoover Institution Press, 1981.

Gunston, Bill., Consultant Editor. The Encyclopedia of World Airpower. New York, New York: Crescent Books, 1980.

The International Institute for Strategic Studies. The Military Balance: 1982-1983. London, Great Britain: The International Institute for Strategic Studies, 1982.

_____. Strategic Survey 1981-1982. London, Great Britain: The International Institute for Strategic Studies, 1982.

Jacobsen, Carl G. *Soviet Strategic Initiatives: Challenge and Response*. New York, New York: Praeger Publishers, 1979.

Johnson, Maxwell Orme. *The Military as an Instrument of U.S. Policy in Southwest Asia: The Rapid Deployment Joint Task Force, 1979-1982*. Boulder, Colorado: Westview Press, 1983.

Kanet, Roger E. "East European States." In *Communist Powers and Sub-Saharan Africa*, pp. 23-56. Edited by Thomas H. Henriksen. Stanford, California: Hoover Institution Press, 1981.

Kaplan, Stephen S., editor. *Diplomacy of Power: Soviet Armed Forces as a Political Instrument*. Washington, D.C.: The Brookings Institution, 1981.

Labayle Couhat, Jean, editor. *Combat Fleets Of The World 1982/83: Their Ships, Aircraft, and Armament*. Annapolis, Maryland: The United States Naval Institute, 1982.

Legum, Colin. "Angola and the Horn of Africa." In *Diplomacy of Power*, pp. 570-637. Edited by Stephen S. Kaplan. Washington, D.C.: The Brookings Institution, 1981.

MccGwire, Michael. *Six Hundred Ships: The Navy and National Security, part II: The Cost*. Unpublished Draft, April 1982.

_____. "Soviet Naval Doctrine and Strategy." In *Soviet Military Thinking*, pp. 125-181. Edited by Derek Leebaert. London: George Allen and Unwin, 1981.

Moodie, Michael and Cottrell, Alvin J. *Geopolitics and Maritime Power*. Beverly Hills, California: Sage Publications, 1981.

Ra'anan, Uri, Pfaltzgraff, Robert L., Jr. and Kemp, Geoffrey, editors. *Projection of Power: Perspectives, Perceptions, and Problems*. Hamden, Connecticut: Archon Books, 1982.

Perry, Charles. *The West, Japan and Cape Route Imports: The Oil and Non-Fuel Mineral Trades*. Cambridge, Massachusetts: Institute For Foreign Policy Analysis, Inc., 1982.

Petersen, Charles C. *Third World Military Elites In Soviet Perspective*. Alexandria, Virginia: Center For Naval Analyses, November 1979.

_____. "Trends in Soviet Naval Operations." In Soviet Naval Diplomacy, pp. 37-87. Edited by Bradford Dismukes and James M. McConnell. New York, New York: Pergamon Press, 1979.

Record, Jeffrey. The Rapid Deployment Force and U.S. Military Intervention in the Persian Gulf. Cambridge, Massachusetts: Institute For Foreign Policy Analysis, Inc., February 1982.

Volsky, George. "Cuba." In Communist Powers and Sub-Saharan Africa, pp. 57-83. Edited by Thomas H. Henriksen. Stanford, California: Hoover Institution Press, 1981.

Watson, Bruce W. Red Navy at Sea: Soviet Naval Operations on the High Seas, 1956-1980. Boulder, Colorado: Westview Press, 1982.

Weiss, Kenneth G. The Soviet Involvement In The Ogaden War. Alexandria, Virginia: Center For Naval Analyses, February 1980.

Articles

Bates, Dr. E. Asa. "The Rapid Deployment Force-Fact or Fiction." Journal of the Royal United Services Institute for Defense Studies, June 1981, pp. 23-33.

Bodansky, Youssef. "Soviet Military Presence in Libya." Armed Forces Journal International, November 1980, pp. 89-92.

Borgart, Peter. "The Soviet Transport Air Force: aircraft and capabilities." International Defense Review, June 1979, pp. 945-950.

Braybrook, Roy. "AV-8B Harrier II." Air International, February 1982, pp. 64-68, 102.

_____. "New Roles For The F-15 Eagle." Air International, August 1981, pp. 61-68, 82-83.

_____. "Sea Harrier Fully Operational." International Defense Review, January 1982, pp. 47-51.

"British Harriers Averaged Six Sorties Per Day." Aviation Week & Space Technology, 19 July, 1982, pp. 20-21.

Bulban, Erwin J. "F-16s Deployed to Norway For Environmental Tests." Aviation Week & Space Technology, 11 May 1981, pp. 69-71.

Chambers, Everett A. "Airlift: Finding the Plane to Fit the Mission." Armed Forces Journal International, November 1982, pp. 40-46.

Cherikov, Nikolai. "The Soviet Mi-24 Hind Attack Helicopter." International Defense Review, September 1981, pp 1131-1134.

Clausen, Perrin. "Test Unit Opposes F/A-18 Attack Role." Aviation Week & Space Technology, 8 November 1982, pp. 26-27.

Clementson, Squadron Leader J. "Diego Garcia." Journal of the Royal United Services Institute for Defense Studies, June 1981, pp. 33-39.

Cordesman, Anthony H. "The Changing Military Balance in the Gulf and Middle East." Armed Forces Journal International, September 1981, pp. 52-60.

_____. "The Falklands: the Air War and Missile Conflict." Armed Forces Journal International, September 1982, pp 32-40.

_____. "Power Projection and the War at Sea." Armed Forces Journal International, September 1982, pp. 40-46.

_____. "The Sixth Arab-Israeli Conflict: Military Lessons for American Defense Planning." Armed Forces Journal International, August 1982, pp. 29-32.

"Development AV-8B to Fly in October." Aviation Week & Space Technology, 21 September 1981, pp. 59-63.

Dunn, Keith A. "Strategy, The Soviet Union And The 1980's." Naval War College Review, volume 34, September-October 1981, pp. 15-31.

Everett-Heath, Lt. Col. E.J. "The Mi-24 Hind in an Anti-Helicopter Role." International Defense Review, September 1981, pp. 1147-1150.

Etzold, Thomas H. "Responding to Soviet Intervention in the Third World." Naval War College Review, volume 35, May-June 1982, pp. 25-35.

"F-15s Used for Air Defense Intercepts." _Aviation Week & Space Technology_, 7 June 1982, pp. 68-72.

Gilson, Charles "Some operational aspects of the UH-60A Black Hawk." _International Defense Review_, July 1980, pp. 1067-1074.

Gordon, Michael R. "The Rapid Deployment Force—Too Large, Too Small or Just Right for Its Task?" _National Journal_, 13 March 1982, pp. 451-455.

Griffiths, David R. "F-15 Pilots Cite Need for New Air-to-Air Missile." _Aviation Week & Space Technology_, 2 November 1981, pp. 52-53.

Halloran, Richard. "Pentagon Chooses Crumman F-14 Jet As Navy's Fighter." _The New York Times_, 2 August 1982, pp. 1, 11.

Hanley, Art. "Sharpening the Claws of the Tomcat." _Proceedings: U. S. Naval Institute_, June 1982, pp. 109-112.

Hansen, James H. "Soviet Projection Forces —— Their Status and Outlook." _Armed Forces Journal International_, October 1981, pp. 76-88.

Hewish, Mark. "US Navy League 1982 - weapon systems proliferate." _International Defense Review_, June 1982, pp. 793-796.

Kanter, Herschel. "The Fleet for the 21st Century." _National Defense_, February 1981, pp. 36-40, 65-66.

Kehoe, Captain J.W. and Brower, K.S. "The Kirov." _International Defense Review_, February 1981, pp. 154-158.

_____. "US and Soviet Weapon System Design Practices." _International Defense Review_, June 1982, pp. 705-712.

Komer, Robert W. "Maritime Strategy Vs. Coalition Defense." _Foreign Affairs_, Summer 1982, pp. 1124-1144.

Kyle, Deborah M. "Navy's 34% of FY83 Defense Budget Sustains Hefty Ship/Aircraft Buy." _Armed Forces Journal International_, March 1982, pp. 58-59.

_____. "Russia's Il-76 Transport: Ten Years Ahead of C-X?" _Armed Forces Journal International_, July 1980, pp. 18-19.

_____. "Sealift." Armed Forces Journal International, July 1982, pp. 57-58, 60.

_____. "US Sealift: Dwindling Resources vs. Rising Need?" Armed Forces Journal International, May 1981, pp. 35-37.

Lambert, Mark. "The US Army's Cobra Companies." International Defense Review, September 1981, pp. 1179-1181.

La Monica, Jay. "RDF's 'Bright Star'." The Washington Quarterly, Spring 1982, pp. 113-116.

Lloyd, Alwyn T. "More Fight For The Fighting Falcon." Air International, October 1981, pp. 161-170, 202-203.

Lopez, Ramon. "The US Army's Future Light Infantry Division - a key element of the RDF." International Defense Review, February 1982, pp. 185-192.

_____. "The United States Marine Corps in the 1980s." International Defense Review, April 1981, pp. 433-438.

MccGwire, Michael. "A New Trend in Soviet Naval Developments." International Defense Review, Number 5, 1980, pp. 675-680.

"Marine Harrier Use Wins Interest of Parent Service." Aviation Week & Space Technology, 21 September 1981, pp. 64, 67.

Meyer, Deborah G. "Interview with Major General Carl H. McNair, Jr." Armed Forces Journal International, May 1982, pp. 48-50, 52, 54.

_____. "The Simplicity vs. Complexity Issue." Armed Forces Journal International, January 1982, p. 46.

_____. "What's in the Army's Arsenal of Aircraft." Armed Forces Journal International, May 1982, pp. 37, 40, 43-44, 46.

_____. "What's in the Soviet Helicopter Arsenal?" Armed Forces Journal International, May 1982, p. 42.

Mulquin, Jim. "ARAPAHO Update." Naval Aviation News, April 1982, pp. 20-23.

"Navy, Manufacturer Concur On Fiscal 1982 F-18 Price."
    Aviation Week & Space Technology, 11 October 1982,
    p. 29.

"Navy Secretary Urges Building Balanced Offensive
    Capability." Aviation Week & Space Technology, 31
    August 1981, pp. 44-45.

"Navy Stressing Survival of Fleet in Nuclear War."
    Aviation Week & Space Technology, 8 March 1982, pp.
    50-51, 55-56.

"Navy Testing F-14 in Ski-Jump Launches." Aviation Week
    & Space Technology, 6 September 1982, p. 43.

Ostrich, Ralph. "Aeroflot." Armed Forces Journal
    International, May 1981, pp. 38-39, 42, 44-46,
    48-50, 54-59.

Panyalev, Georg. "The Ram-L Air Superiority Fighter."
    International Defense Review, December 1981, pp.
    1609-1612.

Peterson, Commander C.B., USN. "LSD-41 Under
    Construction." Marine Corps Gazette, October 1981,
    pp. 18-19.

Polmar, Norman. "The U.S. Navy: A New Destroyer Class,"
    Proceedings: U.S. Naval Institute, August 1982, pp.
    122-124.

"Progress Being Made With LCACs." Marine Corps Gazette,
    October 1981, p. 4

"Reagan's Proposed Five-Year Navy Shipbuilding
    Program." Armed Forces Journal International, March
    1982, p. 51.

Robinson, Clarence A., Jr. "Aircraft Modifications to
    Stretch Over Next Five Years." Aviation Week &
    Space Technology, 21 September 1981, pp. 48-51, 54,
    56.

_____. "Backfire Threat Spurs F-14 Upgrading."
    Aviation Week & Space Technology, 30 August 1982,
    pp. 49-52.

_____. "DeLauer Urges Technology Spending."
    Aviation Week & Space Technology, 6 September 1982,
    pp. 257, 259-263.

_____. "Maritime Superiority Goal Keyed to
    600-Ship Fleet." Aviation Week & Space Technology,
    31 August 1981, pp. 38-41, 44-45, 47.

_____. "Soviet Union Defensive Buildup Detailed by Weinberger." Aviation Week & Space Technology, 5 October 1981, pp. 18-22.

_____. "Surveillance Integration Pivotal in Israeli Successes." Aviation Week & Space Technology, 5 July 1982, pp. 16-17.

_____. "USAF Seeks Continued Effort on C-17." Aviation Week & Space Technology, 1 February 1982, pp. 24-26.

Ropelewski, Robert R. "F-14 Performance Up With F101 Engines." Aviation Week & Space Technology, 19 October 1982, pp. 44-45.

Schemmer, Benjamin F. "Budget Cutters Are Only Ones Likely to Win Battle Over C-5B/747F/C-17 Airlift Alternatives." Armed Forces Journal International, July 1982, pp. 38-40, 42-44, 48.

_____. "Exclusive AFJ Interview: Commander in Chief, USAFE, and Commander, AAFCE, General Charles A. Gabriel." Armed Forces Journal International, January 1982, pp. 25-28, 32, 34-36, 38-39.

_____. "LCAC Contract Finally Lets USMC Put World War II Tactics Behind." Armed Forces Journal International, April 1982, p. 80.

_____. "Marine Amphibious Assault Forces Get Big Boost in New Defense Plan." Armed Forces Journal International, April 1982, pp. 78, 80.

"Soviets Deploy Updated MiG-25 Foxbat Fighter." Aviation Week & Space Technology, 7 June 1982, pp. 54-56.

"Soviets Improving Force Mobility." Aviation Week & Space Technology, 21 December 1981, p. 57.

Sullivan, Captain William K., USN. "Now is the Time to: Rethink, Redesign, and Redeploy Naval Aviation." Naval War College Review, volume 35, March-April 1982, pp. 10-17.

Turner, Admiral Stansfield, USN (ret.), and Thibault, Captain George, USN. "Preparing For The Unexpected: The Need For A New Military Strategy." Foreign Affairs, Fall 1982, pp. 122-135.

"US Marine Corps organizes LAV battalions." International Defense Review, February 1982, p. 191.

Williams, John A. "U.S. Navy Missions and Force Structure: A Critical Reappraisal." Armed Forces And Society, Summer 1981, pp. 499-528.

Wood, Derek and Hewish, Mark. "The Falklands Conflict: Part 1: the air war." International Defense Review, August 1982, pp. 977-980.

Zumwalt, Admiral Elmo R., Jr., USN (ret.). "Naval Battles We Could Lose." International Security Review, Summer 1982, pp. 139-156.